TOWARD BALZAC

Direction

The magazine is published quarterly by New Directions, each number being devoted to a single long work by one author, or to a group of his shorter pieces. Proximate issues will feature the stories of Montagu O'Reilly, of M. P. Hutchins, and of Nicolo Tucci. Subscriptions —$2 for four numbers—and orders for single issues—$1.50 each— should be sent to New Directions, 500 Fifth Avenue, NYC-18.

Toward Balzac

HARRY LEVIN

Direction

THREE

PRINTED BY DUDLEY KIMBALL
AT THE BLUE RIDGE MOUNTAIN PRESS
PARSIPPANY, NEW JERSEY

NOTE

This is a sequel to an essay on Stendhal published last year in *Pharos*, the predecessor to the present series. Both essays are conceived as chapters in a larger study of the French realistic novel, *The Gates of Horn*, scheduled for publication next year by the Oxford University Press. Meanwhile I must assume responsibility for the passages quoted in English, which I have translated from the Conard edition of Marcel Bouteron and Henri Longnon. By also mentioning the *Balzac Bibliography* of W. H. Royce, perhaps I may acknowledge a comprehensive debt of gratitude which can later be paid off in detailed footnotes. Though the researches of innumerable Balzacians have been quite commensurate with the immensity and complexity of their subject, they themselves would be the last to maintain that it was now exhausted. And the criticisms of whom but Henry James, by reverting again and again to *The Lesson of Balzac*, invite us to learn further lessons from the same master? It cannot be said of Balzac, as it still can of Stendhal, that he has not been adequately considered in America. The shelves of any second-hand bookshop attest the widespread vogue of his works a generation ago—as well as our casual neglect of them today. Since many of them are thus accessible, and only a few are currently reprinted, we can make the most of the situation we find. It is curiously fitting that so Balzacian an enterprise as the Book-of-the-Month Club should recently have sent its subscribers a book about Balzac—a book which might have been more than an entertaining biography if Stefan Zweig had lived to complete it himself. Some of its readers will do their supplementary reading, it may be hoped, not in the books-of-the-following-months but in the *Comédie Humaine.* Such is the hope, at all events, in which this brochure is issued. With Balzac, as with every great writer, the main thing is to read him. Yet there never was another writer whose intentions and commitments extended so far beyond the text at hand. Hence there may be some use for an interpretation which, while doing less than justice to particular novels, seeks to comprehend the novelist as a whole, and to set his work in its context of ideas and events.

1 *August* 1947   HARRY LEVIN

CONTENTS

1. THE LAW OF DISORGANIZATION

Criticism, perhaps because there is so much to be said on both sides of any human situation, tends to pair off the masters of the novel: Dickens and Thackeray, Tolstoy and Dostoevsky, Hawthorne and Melville, Balzac and Stendhal. Against the checks and balances of literary history, Stendhal cuts an eccentric figure. His approach is leisurely and experimental; his originality resists facile characterization; his long suspended achievement comes to a head in two compact novels. These, of course, are the very considerations that have made him an accommodating subject for the initial exercise of our critical method. But it is Balzac who occupies the central position in any account of realism, who claims and earns and duly receives the title of novelist before all others. The overwhelming quantity and the substantial quality of his writing form a monument around which there are no detours. Its impressive structure and its uneven texture are better appreciated from a distance, where Stendhal's writing invites a closer scrutiny. Two such disparate temperaments cannot be viewed through the same focus; two such contrasting talents cannot be measured by the same scale. Each establishes his distinctive atmosphere and prescribes the conditions, typical or special, under which he may best be approached. With Stendhal we have had to piece together fragments and to draw out implications; Balzac is so thorough and so explicit that he simplifies—threatens to oversimplify—the problems of his critics. Comprehensive rather than intensive, deductive rather than inductive, synthetic rather than analytic, his work carries its own commentary. And few lives can be more fully accounted for in works. Few writers have repeated, with such strident conviction, *Exegi monumentum.* . . .

9

Stendhal was so nonchalant an amateur, Balzac so inveterate a professional, that there could be no rivalry between them. Instead there was a clear and consistent meeting of minds, warmly attested by Balzac's review of *La Chartreuse de Parme*. The younger writer, the first to win recognition, was the first to recognize the importance of the elder. If the admiration was one-sided, it was a belated acknowledgment that Stendhal had been the pioneer; for *Le Rouge et le Noir* had made its striking contribution to realism while Balzac was still enmeshed in the fantasy of *La Peau de Chagrin*. But Stendhal's values were unswervingly individualistic, and his particular domain lay within the individual consciousness; only in reverse could he create a society. Balzac, whose values were preeminently social, could put the individuals in their respective places, and—what is more—could set the entire panorama in motion. Ramifying plot to the point where Stendhal had refined character, demonstrating the external consequences of motives which Stendhal had treated introspectively, Balzac became the sociologist of the novel as Stendhal had become its psychologist. The two related modes of interpretation, converging upon the same tract of material from opposite points of view, supplement and corroborate each other. The extremes of liberalism and conservatism join forces to interpellate the *Juste-Milieu*, and to complete an indelible record of French life between the Battle of Waterloo and the Revolution of 1848. The obverse of Stendhal's medallion is Balzac's franc. The other side of Julien Sorel's valediction is Eugène de Rastignac's salute. To Balzac, then, we turn for *L' Envers de l'Histoire Contemporaine*.

Balzac may not have invented the nineteenth century, but he did more than any other writer—as Wilde's epigram implies—to exploit it, to cast its fictional matrices, to coin its literary currency. Unlike Beyle, with his classical inheritance and his eighteenth-century childhood, Honoré Balzac was unreservedly a man of his time. He was born at Tours in 1799, the year that witnessed Beyle's arrival at Paris, as well as Napoleon's coup *d'état*. Grandson of peasants and shopkeepers, a son of a clever laborer who had entered petty officialdom via the Revolution, Balzac himself rounded out the cycle by marrying into a foreign aristocracy. The half-generation that divides Stendhal from Balzac is a more tangible barrier than the difference between the highest and the lowest bourgeoisie. Stendhal had grown up during the Revolution and served his apprenticeship under the Empire; Balzac grew up during the Empire and served his apprenticeship under the Restoration. Stendhal's work is a critique of the Restoration from the viewpoint of a revolutionary Bonapartist; Balzac's work is a critique of the July monarchy from the viewpoint of a Catholic royalist. The Restoration, for better or worse, had waved a flag over the ship of state, and concealed the cargo by certain moral ideas and patriotic gestures, as Sainte-Beuve pointed out in a notable essay, *De la Littérature Industrielle.* With the final collapse of the old order, the flag was hauled down, the cargo revealed, and the merchandise offered for sale. Guizot's invitation, *Enrichissez-vous,* was the slogan of the new regime, the text on which the *Comédie Humaine* provides a running comment: "It is a mistake . . . to believe that King Louis-Philippe reigns, and he is not deceived on that point. He knows, as we all do, that above the Charter is the holy, venerable, solid, amiable, gracious, beautiful, noble, young, all-powerful five-franc piece!"

Writers have always held money in mingled esteem and contempt, but never have its attractions and repulsions been more powerfully grasped, for Balzac was at once the notorious victim of industrial literature and its most enterprising entrepreneur. From his earliest transactions on Grub Street to his presidency of the *Société des Gens de Lettres,* he frankly looked upon authorship as a business. "We have no more works," he informs the reader of *Béatrix,* "we have products." George Lukács, describing *Illusions Perdues* as the *Don Quixote* of bourgeois illusions, has aptly stated its theme: the transformation of literature into goods. Hence this novel, a pivotal installment of *La Comédie Humaine,* swings from one to another of its heroes, *Les Deux Poètes.* The poet, Lucien de Rubempré, sets out for Paris with a romance in the manner of Scott under his arm, and is gradually corrupted by the seductions of metropolitan journalism. The printer, David Séchard, perseveres at Angoulême, and invents a paper-making

11

process which is exploited by others. Now Balzac, who can be closely identified with both *Un Grand Homme de Province à Paris* and *Les Souffrances de l'Inventeur*, had tried to be both a poet and a printer, and had hoped to make his fortune by just such an invention. Many times he retells the parable of the idle and industrious apprentices, and he usually allows the credits to accrue on the philistine side of the ledger. In *La Maison du Chat-qui-pelote*, one of the preliminary sketches for his great design, the draper's older daughter marries the industrious apprentice, who inherits the shop and lives happily ever after; while the younger sister marries an artist and comes to grief.

Thus the romance of art is tempered by the realism of business. In another generation, Flaubert's generation, the artist and the bourgeois will agree to disagree. Balzac's realism avoids that issue by making a business of art and by dramatizing the romance of business. It pays the stiff surtax that no artist can avoid when he commercializes his talent; but it succeeds in taking an inventory of the bourgeoisie while their stock is at its height, and in painting as rich and massive a Dutch interior as Théodore de Sommervieux's exhibition picture of the *Chat-qui-pelote*. Balzac condenses his tribute to Scott into a punning epithet: *ce trouveur* (*trouvère*) *moderne*. The modern troubadour, the poet of today, must likewise be a discoverer, an inventor. The Laird of Abbotsford, though he dissembled his enterprises as long as he could, was a novelist and a publisher too. The shadow of bankruptcy, which darkened the end of Scott's career, hung over Balzac's from the very beginning. Happily for Balzac, financial failure was the beginning of literary success. The middle decade of his fifty-year span was his period of apprenticeship and discovery. In his twenty-first year he left a law-office to devote himself to writing. Discouraged in his more ambitious efforts, notably a tragedy about Cromwell, he devoted himself to hack-writing. He turned out, under various pseudonyms, more than a dozen slap-dash novels of the Gothic school. When these fell short of the popularity that would have been their sole justification, he sought more direct ways and means of boiling the pot. He set up shop as a printer and publisher.

12

Printing everything from patent-medicine advertisements to one-volume editions of the classics, he soon branched out into type-founding and paper-making. He soon got into debt. In 1828, through the aid of his family and friends, a petition in bankruptcy was narrowly averted. After that, though he operated in other fields on an increasingly bullish plane, though his extravagances became proverbial, though he barely managed to stay out of the debtor's prison at Clichy, he was never quite solvent. He spent the rest of his life renewing his notes, postponing his bills, and writing his *Comédie Humaine*. "Life is a perpetual loan," explains Mercadet, whose perpetual endeavor to shake off a chorus of creditors is the comic evocation of Balzac's own plight. And, though *Le Faiseur* was the only one of Balzac's plays to be successfully performed, Balzac did not live to see the performance, or to hear the triumphant tag-line that his collaborator, Adolphe Dennery, had added: "At last I am a creditor!" Balzac was a debtor to the end; the crown of his exhausting labors was not to die a bankrupt. Bankruptcy and solvency were to middle-class morality what dishonor and honor had been in the code of chivalry. "To go bankrupt," declares the miser Grandet, "is to commit the most disgraceful of all actions that can disgrace a man." It meant—in the strict letter of the Civil Code—to be legally humiliated, to be socially ostracized, to be deprived of the rights of citizenship. To regain them against such odds, to rehabilitate one's pecuniary honor, to make good the heraldic device of "paid in full" was remarkable enough to be considered a heroic deed in an age when heroism was largely confined to the theatre.

It is in *Grandeur et Décadence de César Birotteau*, which purports to be "the poem of bourgeois vicissitudes," that the tradesman makes his debut as a serious hero, a Don Quixote rather than a Sancho Panza. The first half of the poem, as its anticlimactic title suggests, does not rise above the serio-comic conventions of the mock-epic. César, a retail perfumer, lays out his advertising like Napoleon planning a campaign; drawing himself up like one of Plutarch's Romans, he delivers a ringing challenge to the manufacturers of Macassar Oil. At his apogee, at the ball that celebrates the opening of his enlarged premises, he is no more

13

than the bumbling parvenu, inflated with mercantile hubris, whose pedigree extends from M. Jourdain to George F. Babbitt. But when his real-estate ventures fail and his notary absconds, when the invoices come in and the notices go out, in the maze of courts, the abyss of poverty, and the slow, steep climb to rehabilitation, he attains a moral superiority. The comedy of the exploiter becomes the tragedy of the exploited. When he dies, "a martyr of commercial probity," and—to the accompaniment of Beethoven's Fifth Symphony—is welcomed by Jesus into heaven, the novel sinks into bathos; but it discloses, at all events, the depths of Balzac's sympathy. He deliberately glides over the counter-revolutionary activities of his historic original in order to stake everything upon the wavering balance of debts and credits. César's accounts are meticulously audited, and legal technicalities are expounded with the pettifogging circumstantiality of a case-book. A dealer in luxuries, and therefore a staunch royalist, César represents the restricted capitalism of the *ancien régime*. The rise of a new class of speculators and promoters is predicated upon his fall; the sharp practice of the Tillets and Nucingens is based on the good faith of such heretofore unsung and now disappearing heroes.

The bankruptcy and rehabilitation of César Birotteau, like the poet-inventor partnership of *Illusions Perdues*, is one of the pivots around which Balzac's intentions revolve. It illustrates that social phenomenon which his philosopher, Louis Lambert, calls the law of disorganization.- "When the effect produced is not in direct relation nor in equal proportion to its cause, disorganization sets in." Ambitions outrun abilities, debits overbalance credits, supply exceeds demand, growth succumbs to decay, and institutions lose their equilibrium. We are depressed by the same sense of toppling hierarchies and unrestrained appetites that Shakespeare envisages in his harrowing descriptions of nature run wild and society out of joint. The portentous symptom of these disorders, if not the disorder itself, was—for Balzac and his contemporaries—the French Revolution. Eighteenth-century thought had culminated in the disorganization of society, according to the Count de Saint-Simon; the aim of the nineteenth century would

14

be reorganization, and the journal of the Saint-Simonians was accordingly known as *L'Organisateur*. Louis Blanc was formulating plans for a labor movement in his famous article, *L'Organisation du Travail*; and Renan was to advance the bland proposal that science, after it had finished the job of organizing humanity, should organize God. *"Organize,"* remarks the Russian Prince in Balzac's *Autre Etude d'une Femme*, " 'Organize' is a word of the Empire which sums up Napoleon completely." It is a word which Balzac's acute German biographer, Anton Bettelheim, has invoked to sum up the prodigious task of shaping the *Comédie Humaine*.

Balzac's collected works, taken in their most grandiose terms, are a titanic attempt to impose a cosmos on the chaos of contemporary life. Every volume, in more intimate terms, is a debt acquitted. In paying off his obligations to society, which itself had been plunged into a state of moral bankruptcy, he was contributing toward its redemption. The threads of vindication, expiation, and rehabilitation are deeply woven into the specific patterns and the collective fabric of the *Comédie Humaine*. Most of its characters have something to live down. The revolutionary executioner, Sanson, for whom Balzac had ghost-written in *Mémoires d'un Paria*, attends a mass for the soul of Louis XVI in *Une Épisode sous la Terreur*. In *L'Envers de l'Histoire Contemporaine* an anti-royalist judge, a Fouquier-Tinville of the Empire, is pardoned by his enemies and enabled to vindicate himself by publishing a monumental work on law and order. More familiar with the corruptions of towns than with the countryside, Balzac exhibits his idyllic and utopian strain in two companion studies, *Le Médecin de Campagne* and *Le Curé de Village*. The protagonist in each case, Dr. Benassis or Madame Graslin, expiates a private sin by setting up a model community, a kind of human reclamation project. Dr. Benassis, the mayor of his village, the father of his people, the Napoleon of his valley, whose biography parallels Balzac's, dies in the crucial year of 1829. Madame Graslin, like the protagonist of *Crime and Punishment*, submits to a public confession; but works transcend faith in Balzac's ethical system—"the gospel in action." The Marquis d'Espard, in *L'Interdiction*, acquits a long-standing debt of honor by writing and

15

printing an illustrated history of China—one of the ill-fated publications of Balzac's actual press.

The liquidation of this establishment did not dampen his commercial zest. Whenever he went on a journey, he came back talking of railway shares and canal concessions, timber rights and mining prospects. He could not pass by a manure pile without undertaking to convert it into a gold mine. His friends vie with each other in their anecdotes of get-rich-quick schemes and glibly munificent speculations, improvised and elaborated with the same admixture of the fantastic and the matter-of-fact that animates his books. He drew no distinctions between his literary and his financial interests. He habitually engaged in lawsuits against editors and founded several short-lived periodicals. In his novels he advertised the products of the tradesmen he patronized; he speculated on tickets for his plays; he thought of incorporating his readers into a tontine by combining premiums with subscriptions. Like Defoe, the English novelist he resembles most, he was a man of innumerable projects. None of them, with the all-important exception of the *Comédie Humaine*, ever quite materialized. Taine, as usual, saw the point and overstated it, when he characterized Balzac as "a man of affairs in debt." Balzac was nothing if not a man of letters: literature was his unique means of settling his affairs. His talents and ambitions as organizer, projector, promoter, were finally expressed in his writing. As a writer he was a consummate businessman. Theoretically he could calculate better than James de Rothschild; we have Balzac's word that his publisher, Souverain, said so. We have also the word of Werdet, one of his previous publishers, that Balzac was not a practical businessman. And, to apply the only canon by which such matters can be tested, we have a significant fact: after Balzac's "*Dilecta*," Madame de Berny, had helped to extricate him from the failure of his type-foundry, her son took it over and made a success of it.

Balzac's unsuccessful experiments as a man of affairs confirmed his vocation as a man of letters. It is hard to think of a great writer whose juvenilia are less promising than Balzac's *Oeuvres de Jeunesse*. Although their callow sensationalism per-

16

sists throughout his maturity, they do little to foreshadow his solid accomplishments. "His first operations in mercantile literature," as he candidly termed them, show all of his faults and virtually none of his merits. They bring no new resources to the impoverished conventions of Mrs. Radcliffe and Monk Lewis, Pigault-Lebrun and Ducray-Duminil. Indeed it is only the occasional note of parody that detaches them from the gruesome monotony of their models. Only when *Argow le Pirate* supplies the sequel to *Le Vicaire des Ardennes*, and the sinister pirate reappears in the even more sinister guise of a banker, do we catch a first faint glimmering of the Balzacian vision. But Balzac did not discover his subject, nor adjust himself to his *métier*, until he had been caught in the toils of finance. While Balzac & Cie. was being liquidated, he was rusticated to the wilds of Brittany, where he lived "the life of a Mohican." There, a generation before, during the royalist insurrection of the Vendée, the peasants of the Chouannerie had waged partisan warfare against the Revolution. "They were savages who served God and the King by fighting like Mohicans." *The Last of the Mohicans* had lately been translated and Balzac had begun to regard Fenimore Cooper as the only novelist worthy of comparison with Scott. One was the historian of nature, the other of humanity, as Balzac wrote in a later appreciation. Meanwhile, returning to fiction, he felt that he brought to the imitation of both "a passion and spirit which are present in neither." The lost cause he celebrated was neither the vanishing redskin nor the Jacobite pretender. It was nothing less than the altar and the throne. It was the old order to which— brooding over his troubles, and ascribing them to the new disorder—he came to profess allegiance.

In 1829, at the age of thirty, on the eve of the July Monarchy, Balzac hit his stride with *Le Dernier Chouan, ou La Bretagne en 1799*. Simultaneously, and with equal success, he produced another volume which was to be included in the embryonic scheme of the *Comédie Humaine*. Since Balzac was to be both a romantic *trouvère* and a realistic *trouveur*, his models were to include both the historical novel and the scientific compendium. His casual

17

journalism reflects the taste of the time for facetious monographs and burlesque codes, pompously trifling with such topics as landlords and neckties "considered in their relation to society and institutions." Everything has its physiology, as gastronomes had learned from Brillat-Savarin, whose life and work Balzac recounted for a biographical dictionary. For his own *Physiologie du Mariage* he chose—wisely, in view of his limitations—to emphasize the social institution at the expense of the psychological experience. Compared with the penetrating insight of Stendhal's *De l'Amour*, or the thoroughgoing esthetic naturalism of Remy de Gourmont's *Physique de l'Amour*, it can hardly be taken seriously. To advise other men not to marry unless they have dissected at least one woman is all very well for an irresponsible bachelor, but it holds up a standard of rigorous empiricism which can hardly be fulfilled by any of his novels except *Les Célibataires*. A sequence of married mistresses, over whom his biographers archly linger, seems to have mitigated his bachelorhood. If he could not write of love, as Lytton Strachey asserts, it was not for lack of first-hand acquaintance. It was rather from a strongly masculine tendency to reduce love to sex, to be less interested in the psychological variables than in the physiological constants, to be less at home in the boudoir than in the smoking-room. The complicated liaisons of the *Comédie Humaine* are less convincing than the single-minded *fabliaux* of the *Contes Drolatiques*.

In 1830 the hero of *La Peau de Chagrin*, having gambled away his last sou, wanders along the Quai Voltaire in suicidal mood, when he chances upon a magic talisman which renews his lease on life. Similarly Lucien de Rubempré, dangling on the brink of suicide at the end of *Illusions Perdues*, is rescued by the mysterious Vautrin and launched upon the incredible adventures of *Splendeurs et Misères des Courtisanes*, which waft him from the *haut monde* to the *demi-monde* and back to suicide in 1830. The reprieve from folly, the vicarious existence, the posthumous and anonymous career figure again in the story of Balzac's feminine namesake, *Honorine*—as they do in *Wakefield*, Hawthorne's story of an "Outcast of the Universe." Such were the last twenty years

18

of Balzac's own career, desperately preoccupied with the creation of the *Comédie Humaine*, or more precisely with the hundred-odd novels and tales that constitute about two-thirds of the projected series. Like Vautrin, he led many lives beside his own; he "realized the German superstition of the Double by a phenomenon of moral paternity." Like Ferragus, the proscribed father, he exercised an invisible supervision over his progeny. Since he had no legitimate children, since his single hope for flesh-and-blood immortality seems to have been still-born, he satisfied his paternal instincts by peopling his books with more than two thousand different characters. By creating, as critics say, a world of his own, with the most lavish demiurgy that any artist has ever practised, he gratified his worldly ambitions. In the preface to *L'Histoire des Treize*, he speaks of the satisfactions of playing God. In one of his penny-dreadfuls, *Le Centenaire*, he attributes the longevity of his Faustian protagonist to a vital fluid. That essence, as he enumerates its effects, seems to contain the innermost secret of the artist's powers:

> Today clothed in the rags of misery, tomorrow travelling in a magnificent carriage under the title of an extinct family; saving the lives of the good and condemning the bad men to death; such a man takes the place of destiny; he is almost a god on earth! . . . He holds in his hands all the secrets of the art of government and the secrets of every state; he learns at last what to believe about religions, man, and institutions. He looks upon the vain debates of this earth as from the height of a cloud; he wanders in the midst of the living like a sun; finally he traverses the centuries without dying.

This, we may say, is the hollow reverberation of Arlincourt's *Solitaire*, the fustian journeywork of a self-subscribed "public writer and French poet at two francs a page." Yet it does not exaggerate the ultimate range of Balzac's ambition. Napoleon, through conquest, had dominated Europe; Cuvier, through science, espoused the globe; O'Connell, through politics, embodied a peo-

19

67851

ple. Balzac aspired, through literature, to equal the immensity of those three careers, and to leave a comparable mark upon the century: "As for me, I shall have borne a whole society in my head." Paul Bourget, hailing Balzac as "our literary Napoleon," corroborates this boast. Certainly a Napoleonic complex has never been harnessed to a more constructive purpose. The motto Balzac inscribed under his bust of Napoleon, "To finish with the pen what he started with the sword," suggests a very different task of organization. Scènes de la Vie Militaire, for obvious reasons, is the weakest and most fragmentary section of the Comédie Humaine. "The Napoleon of the People," a folk-tale recited by an old soldier to a group of peasants in Le Médecin de Campagne, is one of the finest chapters in the imperial legend; it is also one of the most elegiac. "No more eagles." The short story Adieu, pathetically re-enacting on French soil the Grand Army's crossing of the Beresina, is a farewell to all that. There is no homecoming for Colonel Chabert, who has legally been slain at Eylau, and whose remarried wife hounds him back into an asylum. As for Philippe Bridau, the half-pay officer of La Rabouilleuse, he returns from a veterans' utopia in Texas, the Champ d'Asile, to outswagger the chevaliers d'industrie of the Restoration and the July Monarchy. Nucingen and Keller—in other words, Rothschild and Laffitte—are now the marshals of France, "massing their securities as Napoleon massed his troops." And action means stock in a corporation.

As for the younger generation, the children of the century, the Napoleonides, "of the same race but somewhat degenerate," who has canvassed their situation more authoritatively than Balzac? Where Stendhal had chronicled an exceptional case, it was Balzac who codified the rules. Stendhal had been a soldier and a diplomat where Balzac had been an unsuccessful businessman, but Balzac was—what Stendhal was not—a successful author. Balzac was compelled to use his imagination where Stendhal could rely on his observation. And where the gregarious Stendhal was an intellectualist, the solitary Balzac—to cap the antithesis— was absorbed in physical things. Instead of living his books, he lived in his books—a sedentary mode of existence for a man of Napoleonic energies. Small wonder that he so frequently reverts to the theme of a double life, or that even his crudest fantasies possess a vitality of their own. Since he had begun his battles, he mock-heroically boasted, several chairs had been shot out from under him. The fields of action continued to beckon; he was tempted, on several occasions, to be a candidate for the Chamber of Deputies; but he was no luckier in politics than in commerce. His fellow authors repeatedly refused to grant him an official status in the Académie Française, and it was a disappointment not to be awarded the Montyon prize for conspicuous virtue. There was never any time for regret, however; there was always another novel to be written. Writing day and night, from twelve to eighteen hours out of every twenty-four, he might well have sighed, with J. Alfred Prufrock, "I have measured out my life with coffee spoons." He shut himself in his room for as long as 26 days at a stretch; he brought out as many as 14 volumes in a single year. By the rule of opposites that seems to dictate most writers' conceptions of themselves, he affected the white robe of a Carthusian. Doubtless he would have been more at home in the Abbey of Thélème than in a charterhouse; but it takes more than affectation to goad a man into blackening so much paper. His debts were his vows, his study was a cell, and composition a monastic regimen.

"Creating, always creating!" he exclaims, in an outburst of complacent blasphemy. "God only created for six days." Between novels there was little rest; there were restless trips to the provinces of France and the corners of Europe. "Constant work is the law of art as it is of life," he moralized over the young sculptor of *La Cousine Bette*. He gave younger writers the terse advice of a self-made industrialist: "Work!" Toward dilettantes and Bohemians and—worst of all—critics he adopted the self-righteous tone of a hard-working craftsman, "a galley-slave to pen and ink, a merchant of ideas." The companionship of women, he warned Gautier, was a distraction to the creative artist. There was no objection to a correspondence, he conceded. "It develops one's style." His love-letters, as we might expect, are voluminous and businesslike. Unlike the unexpectedly intensive revelation of Mé-

21

rimée's *Lettres à une Inconnue*, Balzac's *Lettres à L'Etrangère* merely take us into the wings of the *Comédie Humaine*, and exemplify the austere doctrine that life is at best a dress rehearsal for art. The role of Eve is played, passively and enigmatically, by Eveline Hanska, the cultivated Polish wife of an elderly Ukrainian nobleman. The grand passion that she provoked by a fan letter subsisted for seventeen years on a few brief meetings. In 1850, several years after Count Hanski's death, she consented to be Madame Balzac. Balzac, whose health had been broken and whose output had been declining for two or three years, died in his new home at Paris a few months after their marriage. His labors had killed him at the very moment when his twin objectives, power and pleasure, "to be celebrated and to be loved," might securely have been enjoyed. *Mais il paraît que l'histoire de tous les hommes ne sera jamais qu'un roman pour moi*, he had prophesied in a letter to Countess Hanska. Fiction was his reality. His epistolary romance was consummated in the comic misunderstandings of *Modeste Mignon* and the tragic frustrations of *Albert Savarus*. The latter, having met his mistress in Neuchâtel as Balzac had done, writes a novel about her; but the caprice of fortune—or rather of another woman—keeps them apart, and he ends in the lonely obscurity of the Grande Chartreuse.

It was as if Balzac, like one of his characters, had struck some infernal bargain which empowered him to conjure up a society on condition that he lived and worked in solitude. His biography is a mere calendar of works and days, a tabulation of profits and losses. His interior life has gone into "the perpetual creation that emerges from my inkwell." There is poignance in the fact that the voluptuous setting for the lurid climax of *La Fille aux Yeux d'Or* was modelled on Balzac's own Carthusian study, or that the interrupted love-story of *La Grenadière* was located in a home he had wanted to buy. "I have written my desires, my dreams," he confessed to his Countess. We are not surprised that so many of his characters are monomaniacs when we trace their peculiar obsessions back to their creator's all-embracing megalomania. It is surprising that there has been so little psychological interpretation of Balzac, for few writers have written so unguardedly. His mis-

22

understood geniuses, his unappreciated artists, his persecuted scientists act out the compulsion that bound him to his desk through the nights. His letters refer to his grand oeuvre in the awe-inspiring manner that the Queen's astrologers, in *Le Secret des Ruggieri*, assume when they discuss the philosophers' stone. *La Recherche de l'Absolu* intensifies this note by contrasting the comfortable bourgeois solidity of its Flemish background with the sublimated alchemical quintessence for which Balthazar Claës experiments in vain. The indifferent reception of Balzac's preposterous drama, *Les Ressources de Quinola*, must have seemed a confirmation of its thesis—the obsessive Balzacian thesis of the inventor's sufferings. A contemporary of Galileo's, who has the temerity and the ingenuity to invent the steamship, is forced to scuttle it by the Inquisition. "Hell," he concludes, "is paved with good inventions." Balzac must have touched, in moments of self-questioning, the thin line that separates inspiration from paranoia. To the composer in *Gambara*, and to the tenor in *Massimilla Doni*, their music is divine; to the others it is insane cacophony. The isolated idealists of the *Etudes Philosophiques* stand apart from the social realities of the *Etudes de Moeurs*.

Reality is the never quite attainable absolute toward which Balzac's laborious researches tend. It is his own fixed idea that he exposes in *Le Chef d'Oeuvre Inconnu*, permitting life itself, in the youthful person of Poussin's mistress, to elude the endeavors of art, personified by the half-mad Frenhofer. Is he an incomparable genius or a self-hypnotized charlatan? His encrusted canvas is dismissed by Balzac as a meaningless daub, and yet the reader is left wondering—until he too seems touched by madness—whether a more percipient taste would not discern some brilliant innovation. Cézanne identified himself with Frenhofer, while Picasso has published a series of illustrations. And Balzac's ambiguities have survived to perplex other writers. For Hawthorne, in *The Artist of the Beautiful*, the masterpiece of a lifetime is a delicate mechanical toy, which the careless gesture of the merest child can crush. For Henry James, in *The Madonna of the Future*, there are further refinements to "that terrible little tale of Balzac's." The

23

hesitant perfectionist, who contemplates his blank easel, while his model waxes buxom and middle-aged, bears a closer resemblance to James than to Balzac. Balzac, after all, has more in common with the ingenious interloper, who takes possession of the impatient madonna and thrives on caricature: "Cats and monkeys, monkeys and cats—all human life is there." The allegory should explain why James, the least Balzacian of novelists, bore wistful homage again and again to "the first and foremost member of his craft." For Balzac specialized in those bustling combinations of material circumstance, so characteristic of the American scene, which had eluded both Hawthorne and James. And Balzac's works were translated and circulated in America on a scale which befitted the mass-production of the brothers Cointet or the super-salesmanship of a Gaudissart. To represent the bourgeoisie so thoroughly is to retain certain defects of their qualities, and Balzac remains, far more obviously than Goethe, an inspired philistine. By way of compensation, he can claim with Mercadet: "They will never put a stop to speculation. I have known my epoch." It is often ambiguous, as we try to follow the curve of Balzac's speculations, whether he belongs with the Mercadets or the Galileos. But to run up a perennial deficit into one of the most amazing success stories in the history of literature is to be paid in kind.

24

2. DOCTOR OF SOCIAL MEDICINE

Balzac's professionalism, like Scribe's, owes something to legal training. The future novelist and the future dramatist, while learning to brief human nature, clerked side by side in the office of Guyonnet de Merville. That well-established attorney, under the name of Derville, handles the affairs of many characters in the *Comédie Humaine*. "There are three men in our society, the priest, the physician, and the man of justice, who cannot esteem the world," he tells his client in *Le Colonel Chabert*. "They have black garments, perhaps because they wear mourning for all the virtues, all the illusions." And the country doctor, Benassis, talking to the Abbé Janvier and the justice of the peace, defines their respective functions: "One cures the wounds of the soul, another those of the purse, a third those of the body. They represent society in its principal terms of existence—conscience, property, health." Not that they always live up to Balzac's ideals. Consider the shyster Fraisier and the quack Poulain, picking at the bones of Cousin Pons; or the clerical intrigue of *Le Curé de Tours*, differentiated from the milder ironies of Trollope's *Warden* by all the rigor and ardor that differentiate Roman Catholicism from the Church of England. But Balzac, in his recoil from big business, put his faith in the old-fashioned notary, the exemplary curate, and the family doctor; their acute sense of social responsibility was good for what ailed him and his contemporaries; he envied their professional competence to play the detached and ubiquitous witness, to judge life by a set of clear and distinct principles, to reconstruct what others had destroyed. Viewed in this light, his books are law-cases, cases of conscience, case-histor-

25

ies. His *opus magnum* is a codification, a confession, a diagnosis.

Having begun his career as a lawyer's clerk, he subsequently draped himself in monkish garments, and was eventually greeted by Sainte-Beuve as "a somewhat medical confessor," whose profession gave him access to the alcoves and the alleys, and enabled him to shock his readers by invading privacies and unveiling secrets. Law and religion, he soon discovered, were more honored in the breach than in the observance. This is the sort of discovery that realists are always making; but Balzac, in setting conditions as they were against conditions as they should be, established a clinical method. He associated the writer's function with the surgeon's in *Madame Firmiani*, and prefaced *Les Parents Pauvres* by proclaiming himself "a doctor of social medicine." His most eminent practitioner, Dr. Horace Bianchon, appears in twenty-five stories, almost with the regularity of a trademark, as confidential adviser to the other characters and plenipotentiary of the author. The novel has frequently profited from an association with medicine, for both combine science with art in varying proportions, and each submits an opportunity for observation to a technique of analysis. Rabelais, Goldsmith, and Chekhov are not the only physicians who have enriched the domain of fiction, and Balzac is not the only novelist whose books contribute to what he terms "The Pathology of Social Life," although he is indeed the main contributor. He is rather a social pathologist than a pillar of state or the church; but we shall not appreciate his scientific and artistic views, or his conception of the *Comédie Humaine*, until we have considered his political and religious assumptions. These cannot be separated, inasmuch as Balzac's premise is the conclusion of Bonald's *Théorie du Pouvoir*—the necessity for the throne and the altar.

Bonald and Joseph de Maistre, "those two eagles of thought," had undertaken to answer the *philosophes*, to point the moral of the Revolution, and to formulate a counter-revolutionary philosophy. Balzac was more sympathetic to the somber logic of Bonald, who recommended a Bourbon restoration along imperial lines, than to the ultramontane fervor of Maistre, who looked beyond

26

the monarchy to the papacy. Bonald had been the first critic to call literature an expression of society; Balzac was the first writer to set up this axiom, consciously and conscientiously, as the touchstone of his own intentions. The revolutionary argument habitually appealed to the state of nature; the reactionary answer was an appeal to the concept of society. It was society, Dr. Bianchon noted in the album of *La Muse du Département*, which brought out the two-edged distinction between a water-bearer and a Napoleon. Rousseau had extolled the goodness of natural man because he lived under repressive institutions. Bonald, living through the experiments that swept them away, was more painfully conscious of the unconstrained egoism that reigned in their place. Citing these ethical alternatives in the *Avant-propos* to the *Comédie Humaine*, Balzac declares that man is neither good nor bad; that society, far from depraving him, improves and perfects him; that royalism and Catholicism form a complete system for the repression of his depraved tendencies. Thereupon he makes a famous declaration: "I write in the light of two eternal verities, religion and monarchy." The question then arises, which he anticipates, why evil prevails in his work. It cannot be met by instancing virtuous characters, since the Birotteaus and Eugénie Grandets are usually the victims. It can only be understood as a sweeping moral condemnation of a system, or default of system, which loosens restraint and encourages depravity. Not until the age of William Saroyan would a *Human Comedy* be possible in which pure goodness prevailed.

When the disorder is so serious that nothing good can be expected, it is well to know the worst, and not to blame the doctor for the disease. Balzac's treatment is a kind of literary homeopathy. Thus the social unit, as he repeatedly insists, is not the individual but the family. "The family is society." The trouble, as he twice diagnoses it, is that "there is no family today . . . there are only individuals." Accepting Bonald's fundamental triad of father, wife, and child, he exalts the *père de famille* to the apex; but revolution, undermining the bulwarks of authority, has guillotined him, has cut off the head of the family.

27

La Rabouilleuse illustrates this thesis by depicting both a widow's household and an unmarried *ménage*, and expressing the degeneration that results from the absence of a father. But where are the benefits of his presence? What are the paternal virtues? The avarice of Père Grandet or the weakness of Père Goriot, the lechery of Baron Hulot or the madness of Balthazar Claës? Again the prescription is homeopathic, confronting evil with evil. Now and then, as in *Mémoires de Deux Jeunes Mariées*, a good example is brought in to moralize upon a bad one. Renée de Maucombe consents to a marriage of convenience, raises several children, and quietly reads Bonald; while Louise de Chaulieu is married for love, successively to a foreigner and a poet, and leads an adventurous, unhappy, and sterile existence. Her letters make up the larger and more interesting part of the tale. Balzac's usual mode of presentation is that of an object-lesson, with the lesson lagging far behind the object. The lesson is presented didactically, the object represented dramatically. The medicine is applied externally. There is too much protest, too often in Balzac's own person, on behalf of his eternal verities; while the foreground is occupied, to greater advantage, by all sorts and conditions of sinners against them. The *Comédie Humaine* is essentially a collection of bad examples, like Dante's *Inferno* or Madame Tussaud's Chamber of Horrors.

Not the most incorrigible hater of fathers and families, not Samuel Butler himself, could have treated them more grimly. Yet bankers and courtesans, spawn of the very disintegration he laments, he glorifies. And when he attempts to glorify virtue, to dramatize his doctrines, to modernize the *Imitatio Christi*, he fails—how completely we may gage by comparing his *Médecin de Campagne* with Lamennais' *Paroles d'un Croyant*, which also appeared in 1833. Both writers would have agreed with the Abbé Janvier's definition of Catholic communion as "the image of universal social communion;" but the Christian socialist was backing away from the altar, because he had not found it there, even as Balzac was approaching, because he had not found it elsewhere. He had started from Voltairean rationalism, which he expounded in an epistolary novel, not printed until recently, *Sténie, ou Les Erreurs Philosophiques*. Along with diverse early articles, he had published an "impartial" history of the Jesuits, and tried his hand at a drama about regicide, while these were particularly explosive subjects. While the legitimate dynasty and the Catholic church were still in power, he does not seem to have taken much satisfaction in them. Like a good bourgeois, he detested Charles X and welcomed the Glorious Days. Having been more or less liberal during the Restoration, he became increasingly conservative under Louis-Philippe. He adopted the aristocratic particle *de*, to which he had no claim: his father's surname, before it was assimilated to that of the seventeenth-century letter-writer, had been Balssa. As elder son of a widowed mother who showed an obvious partiality for his scapegrace brother, he sharply sympathized with the royalists on the mooted issue of primogeniture. His failures, as their candidate for deputy, confirmed his distrust of democratic elections.

But it is not fair to attribute his legitimism to snobbery, or to trace his principles—as does his latest biographer, André Billy— to his titled mistresses. Balzac's reaction is primarily a reaction against the July Monarchy, a gesture of opposition, a frame of reference. In *Jésus-Christ en Flandre*, dated a year after the Revolution of 1830, he takes his stand. The drift of the allegory is that nothing short of a miracle can now rescue society from its sinking boat. When his vision is over, the narrator wakes up in a church, and concludes: "Believing is living. I have just watched the funeral procession of a monarchy. The church must be defended!" Perhaps the most pertinent comment upon this credo is a letter to Countess Hanska in which Balzac professes himself a Catholic "politically." Her Catholicism, he writes again, is poetry; and again, his own religion is "wholly terrestrial." This smacks of formalism, like the empty carriages at Goriot's funeral—a device repeated in Gogol's *Dead Souls* and Dicken's *Bleak House*, where outworn institutions are satirized. And Balzac seems to be satirizing himself, when he allows the Duchesse de Langeais to assert: "Religion is intimately allied to property . . . Priest and King

29

are you and I and the Princess, my neighbor—in a word, all the personified interests of the best people." Religion, for Balzac, is a code of morality; for his Duchess, going a step farther, it is a code of immorality. She might be enunciating the clerical opportunism of Julien Sorel, or the Catholic atheism of the *Action Française*. The difference between these varieties of religious experience and Balzac's emerges from *La Messe de l'Athée*, where the atheistic surgeon Despleins, one of Balzac's saints, orders masses to the memory of a pious water-bearer—by way of discharging a debt. What matters, then, are not the articles of belief, but principled patterns of behavior: not the controversies of theology nor embellishments in the manner of Chateaubriand, but a unique means of counteracting the forces of self-interest.

Hence Balzac displays, not the intolerance and fanaticism that agitate later exponents of his creed, but a true catholicity. A favorite pattern, the reunion of opposites, is exemplified by the warm friendship of Daniel d'Arthez and Michel Chrestien, which runs unbroken through the *Comédie Humaine*. Arthez, a great author and royalist deputy, who looks like Napoleon and sounds like Balzac, is seduced by the Princess de Cadignan, and gradually retires from literary and political life. Meanwhile Chrestien, an intransigent republican, has escaped from her toils, and dies gloriously at the Cloître Saint-Merri in the insurrection of 1832. His similarity to Ferrante Palla helps to explain why Balzac acclaimed *La Chartreuse de Parme* and admired the anticlerical Stendhal. From opposite poles both attack the regime, for Balzac's politics is rather an attack on the house of Orleans than a defense of the Bourbons. If he defends counter-revolution in *Les Chouans*, he also follows Scott's conventions of the generous foe and the enemy lovers. If his position is inconsistent, it is impartial; it has room for extremes, but not for compromises. If the *Juste-Milieu* is an *aurea mediocritas*, it is not a golden mean, but a gilded mediocrity, a government—as Balzac is fond of saying—by "mediocracy." Seeking a vantage-point from which to attack it, he entertained the numerous proposals then in the air, a plurality of possible worlds, including Fourier's socialism. And, despite his final adherence to legitimism, Hugo and Zola and Friedrich Engels unite to hail the revolutionary implications of his books. On the other side, the reactionary historian Thureau-Dangin brands them a pernicious influence, and the church they supported places them on the Index. Extremes meet here with a vengeance.

It would be idle to deny the authoritarian tendency of Balzac's expressed opinions. The striking fact is that, holding them sincerely, he should depict the issues of the day in terms which win the approbation of democrats and radicals. Balzac had one commitment that went deeper than any partisanship. "The opinion of an artist," he says in *Les Comédiens sans le Savoir*, "should be faith in his work." Against such faith as his, mere opinion seems arbitrary and superimposed. The up-to-date apologist for orthodoxy is driven, sooner or later, to paradox. *Sur Cathérine de Médicis* brings together the extremists of the right and the left, starting from a polemic against the France of 1840, and concluding with a eulogy of Cathérine by Robespierre. The destruction of Saint Bartholomew and the Terror of 1793 are justified as necessary preliminaries to construction. The inevitable parallel in Balzac's own fortunes is the liquidation that prepared the way for his constructive labors. But art, single-handed, cannot organize a disorganized society; the best it can do is to expose the sources of disorganization. The chief of these, according to Félix Davin, who wrote the authorized introduction to the *Etudes Philosophiques*, is thought. It is thought which undoes the precocious Louis Lambert. As for the antiquated Baron du Guénic, in *Beatrix*: "Religion and institutions thought for him." Vilfredo Pareto, whose ancestor, the Marquis Damaso Pareto, has a niche in the *Comédie Humaine*, would categorize these opposing influences as "combinations" and "persistent aggregates." People and periods tend toward one or the other, a flair for speculation and innovation or an adherence to custom and stability. Paretan sociology, completing the parodoxical retreat from reason that began with Bonald, vacillates between those "magnificent combinations," intellectual or financial, toward which Balzac's characters strive, and that backward swing of the historical pendulum toward the intuitive and the secure.

31

Such were the cross-purposes at work in Balzac's mind—the gambler's yearning for security, the intellectual's revulsion from the intellect, and the genius of novelty pledged to the service of tradition. He had few occasions to practise what he preached, and formalism means little when the forms are neglected. "I am by no means orthodox, and I do not go to the Roman church," he confessed to Countess Hanska, ". . . Swedenborgianism is my religion." Balzac's Catholicism was too formal, too political, too terrestrial to satisfy his need for a personal theology Seeking to disencumber his ideas of the materialism that was their native element, he veered toward the remote extreme of spirituality. The mystic Emmanuel Swedenborg, who had once been a scientist, had described the streets of heaven and the garments of the angels with a matter-of-fact conviction which could not but impress Balzac. It was the quintessence of Christianity, for Louis Lambert, the sociology of the supernatural. Balzac, however, was better initiated in the diabolic than in the seraphic arcanum; his androgynous angel, Séraphitus-Séraphita, belongs to that cloying school of ecclesiastical decoration which the French call *sulpicerie*; yet he, or she, still manages to dazzle such uncloistered spirits as Henry Miller. Unworldliness was not Balzac's forte. He was "less of a natural mystic than any other great writer," as Aldous Huxley remarked, in the days when he could afford to deal uncharitably with pretensions of that sort. The stories that constituted Le *Livre Mystique* seem improbable rather than miraculous. The theosophy of Swedenborg and the illuminism of Saint-Martin intervene to solve the domestic and financial complications of *Ursule Mirouët*; but here the ghost walks in a Balzacian direction, and reveals the whereabouts of missing bonds.

Mysticism is Balzac's middle term between religion and science. Science, which had fostered Stendhal's skepticism, reinforced Balzac's will to believe: to believe in virtually everything, alchemy as well as electricity, elixirs as well as medicines, angelic hierarchies as well as stock-market tips. His was an age of awakening credulities, in which scientific experiment was a miracle and religious ceremony a convenience. The distance between a Per-

32

rault fairy tale and a Jules Verne thriller was not excessive, as Balzac proved by an early effort, *La Dernière Fée*. Realism, ever since Chaucer cast the horoscopes of his characters, has consulted the scientific auspices of its time. Too often it has been unduly influenced by the pseudo-scientists, who have made the most sensational claims or advanced the simplest explanations. Balzac's characters respond too readily, we must admit, to the animal magnetism of Mesmer the physiognomy of Lavater, the phrenology of Gall, and other outmoded theories. But in the great biological debate, the controversy between Cuvier and Geoffroy Saint-Hilaire, which Goethe considered vastly more important than the July revolution of the same year, Balzac saw the issue and accepted the consequences of evolution. Cuvier, though Balzac regarded him as "the greatest poet of our century," had lacked the imagination to conceive how one species could develop out of another. Geoffroy, to whom *Père Goriot* is dedicated, anticipated Darwin by introducing "the principle of the unity of organic composition." The process of composition, of putting fragments together—here was the corollary to Balzac's law of disorganization. If the varied manifestations of nature could be unified by a single hypothesis, what of society? Traditionalists, from Montesquieu to Bonald, had emphasized the natural growth of social institutions. Balzac, as Jean Cassou observes, identified the social order with the natural order. If society was an organic whole, the family was a molecular cell, and the transgressing individual was unnatural as well as anti-social.

Balzac's point of departure, and the basis of his most vivid images, is the analogy between the human race and the animal kingdom. Beneath the literal surface of his narrative lurks a dense underbrush of metaphor, where naked appetites and brute antagonisms snap and snarl. M. Grandet, a leading citizen of Saumur, is as predatory as a tiger and as cold-blooded as a boa-constrictor. *La Vieille Fille* reveals the human molluscs that cling to provincial villages, while *César Birotteau* exhibits the curious lichens that make Parisian roofs their habitat. Marche-à-Terre, in *Les Chouans*, foreshadowing the attributes of Mowgli or Tarzan, is com-

33

pared no less than fifty times to different animals. Balzac pushes the comparison to the point where it becomes a blood relationship, and man himself is firmly linked to the fauna and flora of the naturalists' chain of being. In that strange story, *Une Passion dans le Désert,* a lioness is capable of human emotions; more frequently human beings yield to bestial instincts. After marriage has been reduced to physiology, "the chemistry of the will" invites research. "Look," exclaims Balthasar Claës, as his wife weeps, "I have decomposed tears. Tears contain a little phosphate of lime, some sodium chloride, mucus, and water." Though the decomposition, in this case, was verified by two members of the *Académie des Sciences,* Balzac did not pursue the analytic approach very far. His need, his aim, his method was synthesis. Bankruptcy had taught him the meaning of organization; revolution had taught him the value of dogma; zoology taught him the unity of created things. The doctor, putting into practice what the lawyer and the priest formulated, treated his material as an evolving and expanding organism. In 1834, with *Etudes de Moeurs dans le Dix-Neuvième Siècle,* he served notice on the public that each of his novels was merely a fragment of a more systematic undertaking. By 1842, when the *Avant-propos de la Comédie Humaine* was written, it was already supported by the bulk of his achievement.

The scope of that achievement is vast but not unique, if we bear in mind the productivity of Balzac's period and the gigantism of his literary generation—a generation which, tearing a leaf from Heine's book, liked to dip their pens in Vesuvius. Hugo, Dumas, Scribe, Sue, and George Sand likewise left five-foot shelves of their own works. What distinguishes these from Balzac's is an integrating force, inherent in everything he wrote, which ultimately attains the resonance of a manifesto. The *Avant-propos,* which is not so much a foreword as a postscript, leaves few loose ends. Though its developing structure was subject to many changes, to amplifications and curtailments and revisions over the years, the *Comédie Humaine* adhered staunchly to its basic program. Science alone could not integrate a work of art; Bonald,

Swedenborg, and Geoffroy would have meant little to Balzac if he had lacked a concrete and capacious medium. It was Walter Scott, *trouveur* and *trouvère*, who merited his profoundest acknowledgment, for having "elevated the novel to the philosophic value of history." But the Waverley Novels, which he had long admired for their explorations into "the social movement" of the past, had lacked continuity. Balzac saw life as a continued story, of which each chapter was a novel and each novel an epoch. By coordinating fiction, as Geoffroy had coordinated natural history, the novelist could write social history, could synthesize humanity as Humboldt was synthesizing the cosmos. Stendhal had recognized the psychological importance of environment, but Balzac—following Scott—implemented his descriptions with detailed inventories and atmospheric backgrounds. He even subdivided his *dramatis personae* into men, women, and things, "persons and the material representation that they give to their thoughts." It was Balzac who introduced into literature the physical term *milieu*, which he had borrowed from Geoffroy, and who handed it on to Comte and the sociologists, to Taine and the critics, and to Zola and the other novelists.

Balzac's *Avant-propos*, which introduced the term, was to realism what Hugo's *Préface de Cromwell* had been to the romantic movement. A shift in emphasis, from the drama to the novel and from imagination to observation, had made the writer directly responsible to his enlarging subject. "French society was going to be the historian," Balzac declared, "I had only to become its secretary." Conceiving his task as a problem of documentation, he compiled—in Taine's phrase—"the greatest storehouse of documents that we have on human nature." In his own phrase, he endeavored "to write the history that so many historians have forgotten," that of *moeurs*. He penetrated beyond manners to morals, beyond public events to private lives, by assuming an omniscient curiosity, an omnipresent detachment, and an omnipotent judgment. The doctor attending his patients became a caliph of the *Arabian Nights*, a Haroun-al-Raschid strolling incognito through the bazaars of his modern Bagdad, or—coming closer to

35

home—a Louis XI, "deliberately mingling his royal majesty with scenes of bourgeois life." Did Balzac's fabulous walking-stick confer invisibility upon him, and thereby equip him to gather his stories by eavesdropping? So Delphine Gay alleged in her amusing fantasy, *La Canne de M. de Balzac*. The *Turkish Spy* in the seventeenth century, and Le Sage's *Diable Boiteux* in the eighteenth, had used keyholes and chimneys and similar narrative ruses for detaching the observer and conveying him from one domestic establishment to another. Sebastian Mercier, in *Le Tableau de Paris*, had surveyed the city in the last days of the *ancien régime*; and Etienne de Jouy, in *L'Ermite de la Chaussée d'Antin*, had sketched Parisian habits under the Empire. Restif de la Bretonne, more exhaustively than any of Balzac's predecessors, had approximated the range and liveliness of the *Comédie Humaine*. And the great work did not lack such contemporary rivals as Frédéric Soulié's *Mémoires du Diable* or Eugène Sue's *Mystères de Paris*.

Hugo took a bird's-eye view of the medieval roof-tops in *Notre-Dame de Paris*; in *Les Misérables*, under the modernizing influence of Balzac, he carried his municipal inspection into the sewers. A typical Hugolian vista, a building in the shape of an elephant, betrays his penchant for monstrosities. Balzac is more concerned with the monsters that nestle behind inconspicuous façades, with the hidden treasure in the house next door, the erotic adventure awaiting at the corner. He opens *Ferragus* with an apostrophe to the lights and shadows, the grand boulevards and blind alleys of Paris, "that monstrous marvel, astonishing assemblage of movements, machines, and thoughts, city of a hundred thousand novels, head of the world." Other capitals possess their literary monuments; the London of Dickens and the Dublin of Joyce attract their devotees; but its centripetal attraction makes Paris—for even so late a comer as Henry James— an iridescent jewel, a loadstone of cultural values. Where could a novelist find a more perfect setting for "the thousand and one nights of the occident?" Apartments were beginning to supersede the *hôtel particulier*, cafés and shops were exfoliating, modes and *articles de Paris* exhibiting themselves, *lorettes* and dandies sauntering, tigers

36

and tilburies passing by, all diffusing an air of urbanity which could be encountered nowhere else. All France was divided into two zones: "the province jealous of Paris, Paris only thinking of the province when it needed money." Balzac, acutely aware of this "social antithesis," endowed his work with a geography as well as a genealogy. Surveying Tours or Besançon, Saumur or Angoulême, he showed how post-revolutionary centralization had levelled the old provincial capitals, and he registered the flow of brains and resources toward the metropolis. Paris might be, as he observes in *Melmoth Reconcilié*, "a branch office of hell;" but then, as Leslie Stephen is said to have remarked, hell is the only place worth living in.

It is his own apprenticeship that Balzac recalls in *Facino Cane*, when he speaks of writing in a mansard, taking long walks, and observing forgotten dramas, "admirable scenes, tragic or comic, masterpieces begotten by chance." Among his journalistic pieces are a dictionary of Parisian sign-boards, a treatise on the theory of walking, and other contributions to the pedestrian field of John Gay's *Trivia, or the Art of Walking the Streets*. A group of early sketches is entitled *La Comédie du Diable* and the *Physiologie* calls for a "divine comedy of marriage." *La Fille aux Yeux d'Or*, with its blindfold ride over cobblestones which feel and sound familiar, elaborates the parallel between the infernal circles and the Parisian faubourgs, and promises that the damned souls of the business world will have their Dante. A glimpse of the exiled Florentine himself, brooding over the Ile de la Cité, is the surprise ending of *Les Proscrits*. Just as his *Divine Comedy* subsumed the culture of the middle ages, so Balzac envisages an encyclopedic poem of the "stupid"—the all too human—nineteenth century. The topographical opening of *Père Goriot* issues a Dantesque warning to abandon hope on entering the lower regions. "The peculiarities of this scene, full of observation and local color, could only be appreciated between the slopes of Montmartre and the heights of Montrouge. . . " To us, in our armchairs, the author will present the realistic dramaturgy of metropolitan circumstance. "This drama is neither fiction nor a novel." Lest we remain unconvinced, he adds in English: "All is true." Thereupon the Rue Neuve-Sainte-Geneviève is projected on our minds like an approaching film, and the house of Mme. Vauquer, née de Conflans, is disclosed. We catalogue its appurtenances, outside and inside, and even sniff its *odeur de pension;* we proceed, from room to room and floor to floor, into the lives of its inmates. The plots and counterplots of the drama involve the four estates of Balzacian society: the aristocratic connexion with the Restauds through one of Goriot's daughters, the banking affiliation with the Nucingens through the other, the student life of young Rastignac, and the outlaw existence of Vautrin.

And the different classes, fluctuating with the fortunes of Parisian real-estate, are housed in the appropriate quarters: the upper circles in the Faubourg Saint-Germain, the middle class in the Chaussée d'Antin, the Bohemians in the Latin Quarter, and the underworld in the elusive thirteenth Arondissement. The *Comédie Humaine* has been likened, for sheer heterogeneous inclusiveness, to a department store, to the Tower of Babel, but most aptly to Paris itself. The development of the *roman-feuilleton* and the precedent of the frame-story may have suggested techniques of literary articulation; for Balzac published much of his writing serially, and had started a small-scale collection in *Les Contes Drolatiques.* But the impulse to comprehend a series of individual items within some large-scale collective enterprise was most concretely exemplified by the city, and Balzac's realism was firmly based on its burgher foundations. Had not Cervantes extinguished chivalry with "a written comedy?" he asked. Though he looked with complacency upon Cervantes and Sterne as writers of a single novel, and boasted of having multiplied Richardson's accomplishment a hundredfold, Balzac was still *homo unius libri.* The acts and scenes of his collected works were bound to be incomplete because he had attempted nothing less than to transcribe the spectacle of life in its gargantuan totality—an attempt which one of his prolific successors, Jules Romains, has named "unanimism." Balzac seems to have drawn his actual title from Vigny's *Mort du Berger,* where the poet, eternal spectator, ad-

38

dresses himself to Eva, his personification of nature, impassive theater for the enactment of the human comedy. The aspiration of all poets and novelists toward the stage had been shared by the playwright of *Le Faiseur*. Having once contemplated a dramatization of *The Prince*, and again a Napoleonic redaction of *Don Quixote*, he was in a receptive mood for *La Chartreuse de Parme*. It may even have occurred to him, writing his *Avant-propos* a few months after the death of Stendhal, that the comedy of the nineteenth century was destined to be his own big production.

Balzac's opinion, expounded in *A Combien l'Amour Revient aux Vieillards*, seems to coincide with Stendhal's: "Henceforth our comedies will be narrated. . . . " Books will take the place of the theatre because the bourgeoisie cannot afford to watch themselves being lampooned; Tartuffe has now gone into politics and Turcaret sits on the throne. Louis-Philippe's government, as if to prove this point, had forbidden the performance of Balzac's *Vautrin* because Frédérick Lemaître, in the villainous title-role, had been made up to resemble the Citizen-King. Yet no edict could prevent his subjects from going through their routines, the humour of which could be pointed out to the passer-by. This is literally done, in *Les Comédiens sans le Savoir*, by two of Balzac's irrepressible painters. His sense of the dramatic was keen enough to justify the running title. "Scenes from . . . Life." The scenic, the pictorial, the photographic is a prime element of his craft; his dramatic episodes often give the effect of *tableaux vivants;* and he claims to have foreshadowed Daguerre's invention. In an epoch which had also welcomed the invention of lithography, the comic spirit, inhibited on the stage, won militant expression in the press. There we must seek for the closest analogues to Balzac's talent, for a "pictorial supplement"—in Baudelaire's phrase—to the *Comédie Humaine*. Two caricaturists stand out, in this respect, from an incomparably brilliant generation: Honoré Daumier, artistically the most gifted of all, for his lawyers and laundresses, for *Les Bons Bourgeois Moeurs Conjugales*, and *Croquis Parisiens*, for endless variations on the theme of Don Quixote, and for Robert Macaire; Henry Monnier, whose gifts were rather literary than artistic,

39

for having illustrated *Le Rouge et le Noir*, for having struck the note of realism as early as 1830 in *Scènes Populaires*, for having given an epigrammatic twist to the fatuities of the bourgeoisie, and for having created Joseph Prudhomme. Prudhomme and his creator were to enjoy a theatrical career, and Macaire himself had been adapted from one of Lemaître's successes. They stand together as *bon bourgeois* and *chevalier d'industrie*, persistent aggregate and projector of combinations, as the Sancho Panza and Don Quixote of the period, the prototypes of César Birotteau, Maxime de Trailles, and the heroes and villains of the *Comédie Humaine*.

It was difficult for the novelist not to be a caricaturist, as Dickens and Thackeray were finding under similar circumstances. Balzac contributed verbal cartoons to Daumier's periodical, *La Caricature*, and Daumier delineated his own interpretation of *La Comédie Humaine*. And, if Balzac had borrowed some traits of Birotteau from Monnier, Monnier was to return the compliment in *Grandeur et Décadence de Joseph Prudhomme*. The truth, we may suspect, is that their shrewd eyes were fixed on the same models, and that the picture society offered—in the words of the Duchesse de Beauséant—was an assembly of rogues and fools. To effect a comic demonstration of this truism, a reversion to type of characters who had other pretensions, a denouement in which everybody got fleeced, was the trick of Balzac's trade. The money-bags of Harpagon, the stratagems of Sganarelle, the jealousies of Géronte, the impertinences of Toinette, the lovers, whatever their names were—could it be the same old troop, forced to improvise, over and over again, the well-worn scenarios with an occasional change of costume? Balzac enjoys bringing out the resemblance of a detective to Figaro, a salesman to Scapin, and other figures to their counterparts in the classical repertory. The epithet *Molière médecin*, when we remember Molière's notorious distrust of doctors, is paradoxically apt; but Balzac's medicine is stronger stuff than the horrendous purgatives of Dr. Diafoirus. The social comedy consists of many individual tragedies: Goriot's agony is a cynical lesson for Rastignac. The relationship between age and youth is one of the subtlest lines that Balzac traces, since it leads us into the middle age of the century. For the youthful romanticist, life is large, albeit fragmentary; for the adult realist, the astronomical perspectives have scaled down to convenient landmarks. Balzac's world is ultimately a small one. How else could he have managed to set it all down? Familiarity with it breeds contempt for it. The astringent experience it holds for us, which Baudelaire has so poignantly caught, is the shrivelling—from the Titanic to the Lilliputian—of a generation's values.

> Pour l'enfant, amoureux de cartes et d'estampes,
> L'univers est égal à son vaste appétit.
> Ah! que le monde est grand à la clarté des lampes!
> Aux yeux du souvenir que le monde est petit!

3. SUBTRACTING THE DISCOUNT

If disorganization was the cause of Balzac's troubles, his peculiar sort of unified composition was the cure. We have seen his project assigned to him by circumstances, and have tried to conceive it—and them—in his own terms; we have annotated his preface by glancing at his table of contents. The plot and characters of the human comedy, the methods and results of his component "studies," their contribution to the technique of realism and their transcription of social history are the matters that concern us further. Magniloquently heralded and hastily composed, there was bound to an immeasurable gap between the conception and the execution of the *Comédie Humaine*. Organization, for Balzac, meant all-embracing inclusion rather than discriminating selection. As secretary of society, it was his duty to describe exhaustively and his privilege to digress sententiously. His inevitable failure to complete the survey, to exploit every claim he had staked, is more excusable than the effort to incorporate a number of stories and episodes which were hardly worthy of his maturing plans. Few great structures have been filled out with so dangerous a proportion of rubble. If only Balzac's style had lived up to his conception, sighed Lamartine, then France would have had another Molière. That Stendhal should have asked Balzac for stylistic advice is one of the ironies of their relationship; for Balzac carries the traditions of French prose to a demotic and somewhat overripe stage, while Stendhal initiates the modern revulsion from rhetoric. In a revealing letter to Countess Hanska, Balzac defines style as "a garment"—in other words, as something which can be put on or taken off at will, like his monkish dressing-gown.

Style, in his case, is not the man himself so much as the

exigencies that pressed him. His debts could only be floated by accelerating his rate of production. The *mot juste* is necessarily the fruit of leisure, and Balzac did not write—complains Thackeray —"like a gentleman." He once planned to turn out a novel a month and, though no one could have maintained that deadline for very long, he met and surpassed it on numerous occasions. *Cèsar Birotteau* was written, rewritten, and on the press in twenty days. The pen that dashed off *Le Secret des Ruggieri* in a single night could never have hesitated an instant nor blotted a line. It was as if the organic process of writing had been caught up in the mechanical process of printing. The roughest of drafts went, chapter by chapter, to the compositor, and came back over and over again for revision in proof. An endless and illegible sequence of printer's corrections broke into the galleys as often as twenty times, and all but consumed the profits the author had counted on. What was worse, he acquired the habit of interpolating and elaborating, of separating the substance from the form of his work, of applying the style to the surface by a process of overlay. Sometimes it seems to be laid on pretty thick, with a display of allusions and a bandying of epithets which leave the reader feeling like Macaulay's schoolboy. Balzac's imagery, which Taine has sharply scrutinized, is "a gigantic chaos;" and yet that chaos, like the encyclopedia, is somehow organized. "Chemistry expounds love, love borders on politics, music or cookery is related to philosophy." Nothing human is irrelevant to Balzac; everything is related, deviously if not directly; in tracing those relationships, through whatever channels they may lead, he is at his best.

He is at his worst when he conjures with names or airily mentions works of art, in the naive hope of enhancing his artistic tone. He reaches the nadir of taste in the hypertrophied last sentence of *Massimilla Doni*, where muses, angels, sylphs, and a varied assortment of famous madonnas are invited to lament—at the foot of his heroine's bed—her departing virtue. In effectual contrast, because it runs closer to Balzac's vein, is the metaphor that runs through *Le Cousin Pons*: "Let us borrow an image from the railways, if only to compensate for their borrowings from us

44

. . . " Society is envisaged, as in Tennyson, "Launched on its metallic path with the swiftness of a locomotive." Despite his metaphorical intimations of wildness hiding behind tame exteriors, Balzac remains the inveterate city-dweller, embarrassed at being confronted directly with nature. Confronted with the scenery of his native Touraine, he crowds fifteen figures of speech into the first page of *Le Lys de la Vallée,* and suffuses a hothouse atmosphere. He is more at home with landmarks than with landscapes, utterly fascinated by street scenes and domestic arrangements, anxious to bring household interiors and family groups within the range of his flashlight photography. If Barbey d'Aurevilly complained that Balzac made description "a skin disease of the realists," if Flaubert campaigned for a more rigorous selectivity, it was because Balzac had managed to reproduce so many familiar objects, to put so many recognizable sights into words for the first time. Exuberance clutters his narrative with Homeric catalogs and Rabelaisian lists; two steps forward and one step backward is his regular pace. But there are frequent variations, largely colloquial, when he stops speaking and lets us listen to his characters: their smart table-talk and shrill curtain-lectures, their genial *blague* and surreptitious *argot.*

Dramatic dialogue and photographic description, relieving and highlighting what James calls "foreshortened" narration, often lend the effect of solidity to flimsy materials. Balzac faced the handicap of having learned his profession in an undistinguished literary school. His apprentice novels, as a historian of the *roman noir* reminds us, are among the very blackest of the lot. Yet life itself holds secrets which outshadow Mrs. Radcliffe's, we are reminded by the preface to the *Histoire des Treize.* Chance is the greatest novelist, we read in the *Avant-propos;* but Balzac was overanxious to collaborate with chance. When he cast off such youthful pseudonyms as Lord R'hoone and Horace de Saint-Aubin, he did not abandon the disguises, the coincidences, and the sensational conventions of popular fiction. *Une Femme de Trente Ans* reverts to the themes of *Argow le Pirate,* and *Splendeurs et Misères des Courtisanes* is no more credible than *Clothilde de Lus-*

ignan or *Jane la Pâle*. Balzac's firm had meanwhile printed the third edition of Vigny's *Cinq-Mars*, and the *Comédie Humaine* had found reputable models in the Waverley and Leatherstocking volumes. A novel entitled *L'Archer de Charles IX* wins Lucien de Rubempré his brief success as "the ape of Walter Scott," and poor old Cousin Pons misses his opportunity by dying before he can compose the operatic score for Cooper's *Dernier Mohican*. Balzac's hall of fame embraces the works of previous novelists, on which he is constantly drawing for mythological comparisons. Laurence de Cinq-Cygne, the dashing horsewoman of *Une Ténébreuse Affaire*, is another Diana Vernon; Maxence Gilet, the small-town bravo of *La Rabouilleuse*, has the hawklike vision of Natty Bumpo. Scott's influence is gradually neutralized by Balzac's maturity, but Cooper's hold—as we shall see—is annually strengthened.

Challenging Scott on his own terrain—and Balzac's sister tells us that *Maître Cornélius* is a matter-of-fact rejoinder to the intolerable picturesqueness of *Quentin Durward*—he deliberately bases his story on a folk-tale, and solidly builds it around the establishment of a medieval usurer. The characterization that stands out from the wraiths of *Le Martyr Calviniste* is a Balzacian portrait of the sixteenth-century surgeon, Ambroise Paré. *Le Succube*, the most ambitious of the *Contes Drolatiques*, amasses a portfolio of legal documents. By reviving the primordial bourgeois convention of the *fabliau*, Balzac's realism invades the most hallowed regions of romance; though his droll tales show the usual weaknesses of stylistic *pastiche*, they penetrate more deeply into the marrow of the middle ages than any historical novel. His search for better masters guided Balzac to Rabelais, and to their compatriot, Béroalde de Verville, whose *Moyen de Parvenir* was more emulated than imitated. Balzac, however, had not forgotten the lurid vistas contrived by the Gothic novel. No book haunted him more than *Melmoth the Wanderer*, a strange and episodic medley of thriller and sermon, by the Reverend Charles Mathurin. Its Byronic hero-villain, an Anglo-Irish squire, finds many reasons to repent of his pact with the devil, but cannot die

46

in peace until some one else is willing to exchange his hope of salvation for Melmoth's supernatural powers. Balzac's cynical epilogue, *Melmoth Réconcilié*, conveys the aged wanderer to Paris, where his dubious bargain is snapped up at once by the cashier of the Nucingen bank. There the combination to the vault is like the "Open Sesame!" of the *Arabian Nights*; souls circulate, like bills, at increasing discounts, on the stock-exchange; "the principle of honor is replaced by the principle of money."

Melmoth Réconcilié, slight and neglected though it be, is strategic in Balzac's development, for it reconciles fantasy with fact. Up to a certain phase, he can still be regarded as a rival of Nodier, a professed imitator of Hoffman, a specialist in the grotesque and the arabesque. Some of his short stories bear a striking resemblance to Poe's: compare *La Grande Bréteche* with *The Cask of Amontillado*. But motiveless suspense is never sufficient for Balzac; here he motivates the denouement with sexual intrigue and religious irony. The underlying dichotomy of his genius, his alternating dependence on observation and imagination, was pointed out by Philarète Chasles and amplified by Sainte-Beuve. To take Balzac at his face-value was to regard him as an observer and analyst; his romantic contemporaries, like Gautier and Baudelaire, chose to emphasize his visionary side. They considered him, like Louis Lambert, a *voyant*. Max Nordau, pushing this view to the extreme, considers him a somnambulist. If he was dreaming, he kept his eyes open; his hallucinations are distinguished by circumstantial exactitude and pictorial concreteness. "My sole ambition has been to know," says his emissary in *La Peau de Chagrin*, "*Voir n'est-ce pas savoir?*" And believing is seeing, when the mind can project its beliefs into such vivid imaginings; when the inward eye becomes a camera eye, focussed on outer phenomena. Scores of anecdotes vouch for his absorption in the imaginary lives of his characters: "Let us get back to reality; let us talk of Eugénie Grandet." He did not seem to be escaping from the concerns of his fellow men, but rather to be pursuing them with a special concentration. With no responsibilities but debts and no means of expression but writing, he had just enough

47

worldly intercourse to substantiate his dreams and not enough to satisfy his appetites. That he created a vicarious world is not surprising. The surprise is that it should correspond so elaborately to the actual world.

To what extent the foremost of the realists was in touch with reality is obviously the decisive question. Psychologically it is also a delicate question, the investigation of which has revealed little beyond the preconceptions of Balzac's critics. Sociologically we are on somewhat firmer ground, since it is the ground that Balzac himself has chosen. Since he liked to boast of competing with the civil registry, Pierre Abraham is justified in tabulating a statistical analysis of the population of the *Comédie Humaine*. In stature, pigmentation, and other physical traits, they differ exceedingly from what anthropometrists might expect of a few thousand French men and women. In fact, as ordinary readers might expect, the exceptions tend to overbalance the norms. Balzac tends, like any journalist, to take the average for granted and to play up the angles. His account of daily life is exaggerated, like any newspaper. Furthermore, in his busier moments, he is likely to substitute bookish clichés for independent observations. This, of course, is what romancers are licensed to do; but it belies his pretensions as an archivist. Countless dissertations and monographs have retraversed his topography, and assiduously verified his backgrounds. While the professorial sense of reality is not to be identified with the absolute, it guarantees the substantial accuracy and completeness of Balzac's realism on the guidebook level. On the more complicated levels of human behavior, we are forced to admit that some of his personages are more readily encountered in books than in the streets. Of them Howells has remarked: "Balzac, when he imagined these monsters, was not Balzac, he was Dumas; he was not realistic, he was romantic."

But the author of *The Rise of Silas Lapham* begs the question. His kind of realism, the notation of the normal, was inconceivable to Balzac. There was then no ready-made alternative to Dumas, there was only the method that Balzac finally achieved. Both writers started with conventional equipment, an equipment designed for pleasantly adventurous sorties into a romanticized past, and Balzac's problem was to utilize this for the treatment of contemporary society. How he solved it is suggested by Croce's remark that Balzac set the Three Musketeers up in business, endowing his inventors and investors with the spirit of Dartagnan and his dashing companions. By presenting these creatures of romance against a realistic setting, he approximated "le romanesque réel que présente notre société." Life itself was inextricably mingling "those epic elements, the marvellous and the true." Chimeras were changing into realities, as the *Avant-propos* declared; the scientists were outstripping the romanticists. There are times when a grasp of the facts requires an exercise of the imagination, when inventive energies must be measured by wildcat schemes and coffee-drugged fantasies. Though Balzac's projected novel, *L'Histoire et le Roman* was never written, we may safely assume that it would have been another illustration of his major premise—truth is stranger than fiction. The local colorists were calling attention to the dramatic aspects of everyday existence; they went so far as to seek among the common people for heroes and heroines of Shakespearian stature. Russia, for example, would reveal itself in *A Hamlet of the Shchigri District* or *A Lady Macbeth of Mtsensk*. Turgenev was to discover King Lear on the Russian steppes, as Balzac had already discovered him at a French *pension* in the person of a retired noodle manufacturer, Jean-Joachim Goriot.

Balzac is fond of providing his characters with literary precedents. His is not the traditional formula of anti-romance, though he pauses to parody the Radcliffian novel in *La Muse du Département*. Habitually, instead of appealing to realism against romanticism, his technique is to romanticize reality. Like Tartarin, he combines Don Quixote with Sancho Panza. Unlike the deflationary Stendhal, Balzac is in style and temperament an inflationist; he puffs up everything he touches, heightens the commonplace, distorts for effect. The resulting perspective is akin to the grotesquerie of such tragicomic street scenes as Gogol's Nevsky Prospect or Dickens' Chancery Lane. Its feeble imitation is the attempt to convert sordidness into quaintness, as in Murger's *Scènes de la Vie de Bohème*—the very title an echo of Balzac's "scenes from life." Its end-product is the prefabricated fiction of that Broadway Balzac, O. Henry. The secret of the real Balzac's clairvoyance is a genuine and unflagging curiosity about the lives of others. "How lovely it is!" he exclaimed, when Baudelaire showed him a painting. "But what are they doing in that hut? What do they think about, what are their troubles? Have the crops been good? No doubt they have bills to pay." Here, where the shoe pinches, is the Balzacian touch. Bills become as perennially relevant as crops, as universal as death and taxes. A writer whose researches are a method of dramatizing his doctrines is not much of an empiricist; but there is a point in Balzac when life and work, observation and imagination coalesce—the point where the bills come in. "He has learned much, both of good and evil, from observation of facts or contemplation of ideas, but not from experience." So George Sand testifies, forgetting the crucial experience that Balzac could not forget. And since, in a capitalist economy, the dread of insolvency is almost as powerful as the love of money, he may be said to have undergone the cycle of his age.

If—as the dollar-conscious James, among others, has said—the protagonist of the *Comédie Humaine* is the five-franc piece, it is rather the villain than the hero; its ubiquitous and diabolical fascination, rather than any set of proclaimed principles, is Balzac's *moteur social*. The Golden Calf has indeed usurped the altar and the throne. Behind the dynasts and statesmen stand the bankers and businessmen, and behind them—in the very back-room of society—sits the money-lender Gobseck, flashing the mesmeric glance of the Wandering Jew and convulsed in the soundless laughter of Leatherstocking. Passions, "aggrandized by the play of social interests," parade before him; financial experience has qualified him for "the penetration of all the springs that move humanity." Believing in nothing, he is still a poet; for he comprehends the significance of millions, and contemplates the cities and peoples of the earth. And, after his profit has been duly deducted,

50

he retains a harsh integrity, which he vindicates by saving the fortune of the Restauds from the depredations of Goriot's daughter, now the dowager Countess. Gobseck, then, is the devil's advocate, the spokesman of the franc, the Vergilian guide through the fiscal inferno. "Keep your illusions if you can," he advises Derville, a hopeful novice of the law. "I will subtract the discount from life for you." Thereupon he translates the *moeurs* into a handful of trenchant maxims. Moral convictions are valueless phrases; the only valid instinct is self-interest. "Man is the same everywhere. Everywhere the battle between the rich and the poor is entrenched; everywhere it is inevitable. Hence it is better to be the exploiter than the exploited. . . " Everywhere the ego, all is vanity. "Power and pleasure sum up your whole social order." It is money that operates the machinery of life. "Gold contains everything in essence and gives everything in reality."

The sharp theories of *Gobseck* put into sharp practise, supply the plots for dozens of Balzac's other stories. We have recognized that *Père Goriot* is a bourgeois redaction of *King Lear*. But how can so lofty a tragedy be transposed to the middle plane? The answer is indicated by a jotting from Balzac's notes: "A fine man —middle-class boarding-house—600 francs income—despoiled by his daughters who both have 50,000 francs income, dying like a dog." From this meager basis, the plot ramifies into a series of transactions, as carefully audited as Birotteau's. The dying Goriot concludes that "money is life;" the miser Grandet assumes that "life is a business." In the business of exploitation, where Père Goriot is one of the plotted against, Père Grandet is one of the plotters. His name is an anagram of *d'argent*; his philosophy is Bentham's theory of interest; his Midas-touch turns everything into francs and centimes. "Poor young man " cries Madame Grandet, when their nephew's ruined father commits suicide. "Yes, poor," agrees Grandet. "He hasn't a sou." If *Eugénie Grandet* were a comedy like *L'Avare*, the poor young man would end by marrying his rich young cousin. Nor is it a tragedy for Eugénie, since she remains untouched by the means of corruption: the portagues, genovines, Dutch ducats, double Napoleons, and rupees

51

of the Grand Mogul. Her quiet firmness, through the long ordeal of the provincial years, makes her the moral antithesis of Emma Bovary, and explains why Flaubert—who was no admirer of Balzac —held a high opinion of this novel. The really tragic figure is the poor young man, grown rich and corrupt in the Indian slave trade, jilting his cousin and the values she preserves. "He perceived that the best means of attaining fortune, in the tropical regions as well as in Europe, was to buy and sell men."

Going beyond the classical or biblical premise that money is the root of evil, Balzac chronicles—in terms of its impact on hundreds of private lives—the growth and ramification and flowering and blight of capitalism. Swaying with the satirist's ambivalence, he seems to enjoy the cake he renounces, to revel in what he condemns—in Nucingen's deals and Gaudissart's bargains, in Gobseck's usury and Grandet's hoard. When Ruskin asserts that "a miser cannot sing of his lost money," he is overlooking the lyric rapture that coin of the realm can awaken in Balzac. This lyricism, like the romantic prose of the advertising agencies, parodies itself; it inflates itself, like Ben Jonson's verse, in order to become satire. The art-dealer boasts, in La Peau de Chagrin, pointing at Raphael's Christ, "I have covered this canvas with goldpieces." And, under that blasphemous implication, the whole antique-shop depreciates; the jumbled inheritance of the ages is worth no more than a Russian kopek or a Scotch farthing or a Levantine piastre. A sequel, L'Auberge Rouge, reaching back into the career of the millionaire Taillefer, uncovers a murder at the base of his fortunes, and implies that wealth is tainted with original sin. As for poverty, it is always with us, and the odds that favor the exploiter disappoint the exploited. Madame Descoings, in La Rabouilleuse, plays the same lottery number for twenty years, and is robbed on the day it turns up. The religion of Louis-Philippe's charter, which takes nothing into consideration except property, enshrines the money-changers in their temple, the Bourse, and sanctifies a thriving traffic in bodies and souls. Values are pegged to the gold standard, taste is ruled by pecuiary canons. Balzac's shrewd insight affixes to everything its plainly marked

52

price-tag. The cost of passion is computed in taxi fares and tailor bills.

"Gradually the ideas of exchange, of devaluation, of inflation invaded his book, . . where they usurped the place of characters." These words are André Gide's, referring to *Les Faux-monnayeurs*, and to the final discounting of the debased coinage against which Balzac warned his contemporaries. He regretted that property, "the most vividly materialized of human ideas," should be the sole remaining bond between man and man. The running inventory, the interior decoration, the insistent materialism, the visual and tangible and audible detail of the *Comédie Humaine* are his means of subtracting the realistic discount from the gross exaggerations of romance. Attaching as much importance to things as to men and women is his most devastating innovation. "He narrates the ornaments of the chimney-piece, the clock and the candelabra, and they live with strange intensity . . . ," George Moore observes. "There is life in Balzac's hats and neckties." Things are virtually human; humans, on the other hand, are enslaved to their goods and chattels—a lesson from Balzac which James perceptively applies in *The Spoils of Poynton*. Balzac himself was an impassioned collector of bric-à-brac, and some of his prized possessions are catalogued with the collection of Cousin Pons. Like the predatory animals of Jonson's *Volpone*, or—in Balzac's simile—like crows around a corpse, the presumptive heirs flock to the old musician's deathbed. After his third-class funeral, a salesman palms off a tombstone on Pons' faithful colleague, Schmucke. Its three allegorical figures, designed to mark the grave of a politician, were supposed to represent the Glorious Days; proposed again and again rejected as a monument to a banker, they served as the Army, Finance, and the Family; now, for the poor relation, they are Music, Painting, and Sculpture. And *Le Cousin Pons*, the last novel Balzac completed, is his mordant allegory of the destiny of the arts in a commercial civilization.

Flaubert foresaw that Balzac's methods of literal representation—"a novel on chemistry, another on banking, another on the printing press"—would sooner or later reduce novels to monographs. "We shall have them on every trade and on all the provinces, then on all the towns and the stories of each house and each individual—which will no longer be literature but statistics and ethnography." Conversely, no writer would be able to stray beyond his first-hand department without running the risk of journalistic superficiality. Balzac, having taken all society for his province, proves less versatile than his pretensions; his documentation falls short of his program. His visits to battlefields did not result in any full-scale depiction of war. Even his scenes from political life, contrasted with Stendhal's, redound to the advantage of the *livre vécu*. Out of Balzac's disappointments as a candidate, he painted an unfinished picture of carpet-baggers and rotten boroughs in *Le Député d'Arcis*; but his statesmen are not so convincing as his businessmen. We take it on faith that Henri de Marsay has been prime minister; but whenever we meet him, in the pages of the *Comédie Humaine*, he is merely engaged in gossiping or philandering. Faults have been found in Balzac's presentation of the upper classes: his fashionable *milieux* are unexpectedly vague or incredibly flamboyant. It is with the middle class that he is thoroughly at home, and that realism lavishes its gifts on its favorite subject. The lower class is even more remote than the upper: not the proletarian slums, but the lowest depths of the underworld, solicit the romanticist in Balzac. He shares Stendhal's preoccupation with the criminal, Baudelaire's with the prostitute. There is still room, in the interstices between his pavements, for flowers to spring up or abysses to open. He is lured by "the poetry of evil."

The devil in the machine is Jacques Collin, *alias* Vautrin, *alias* Trompe-la-Mort, *alias* the Abbé Carlos Herrera, who emerges from these incarnations as the most dynamic and yet elusive character in the *Comédie Humaine*. When everyone is a villain, more or less, the arch-villain is a hero. In paying his respects to the romantic outlaw, Balzac out-herods his contemporaries and himself. He exhausts the repertory of demonic analogies, from Satan and Cain to Robespierre and Napoleon. Vautrin is literally a marked man; for when the police strip the shirt from his shoulders, the brand of the galleys is revealed. He is also a poet who acts out his poems, an artist in crime as Molière is in literature and Cuvier in science. As a philosopher, he is a disciple of Rousseau, protesting against the deceptions of the social contract. Balzac is less concerned with a credible characterization than with a sinister influence, with the personified temptations that waylay ambitious young men; yet there is more than a hint of homosexuality in Vautrin's paternalistic surveillance of Rastignac, Rubempré, and other protegés. It is in the cards that the reformed convict will go over to the police, and emerge as head of the Sûreté Générale, since Balzac has been following the adventures of the famous detective, Vidocq. Both Stendhal's Valbayre and Hugo's Valjean were similarly influenced by Vidocq's memoirs. Balzac, too, may have been impressed by the Count de Saint-Hélène, the original of Dumas's Monte-Cristo. A significant conversation is on record, in which Vidocq taxed Balzac with evading reality. "It is we who create reality," retorted the novelist. Certainly he preferred his own creations to the commonly accepted versions, as he showed by rushing into the notorious Affaire Peytel. Here we see the realist setting aside the obvious and sordid motives, advancing a far-fetched and highly colored explanation, and convincing nobody that Peytel was not guilty of his wife's murder.

As we pass from the upper and middle worlds into Balzac's underworld, the tragic emotions and the comic machinations are interlocked in melodrama. Good and evil, no longer present as ethical alternatives, are hypostasized into secret societies of not very human beings: either benefactors, like the Confrérie de la Consolation in L'Envers de l'Histoire Contemporaine, or—more typically—malefactors, like the Dévorants in Histoire des Treize. Balzac's suspicious mind, forever deducing causes from effects, traces upheavals to subterranean agencies. Agents and spies are endlessly conniving behind the scenes of the Comédie Humaine. Its plots are plots in more ways than one. As the mere task of fathoming their complications, by deductive methods, becomes an end in itself, Balzac is pushed, like Dickens, in the direction of the detective story; his logical successors are Gaboriau, Ponson du Terrail, and the perpetrators of the *roman policier*. The mystery of *Une Ténébreuse Affaire* is overshadowed by the shady genius of Fouché; royalists and Bonapartists are both double-crossed by the police. The all-seeing and all-knowing policeman is eulogized, in language reminiscent of Maistre's panegyric on the hangman, at the conclusion of *Les Petits Bourgeois*; although this passage was probably added by Balzac's collaborator, Charles Rabou, Balzac had shown himself an old admirer of the guillotine. Above the fallen dynasties, and the corrupted bourgeoisie, looms the survival of sheer amoral power. When Balzac's arch-criminal turns out to be the final incarnation of law and order, when Vautrin's theatrical disguise is the full uniform of Louis-Philippe, values are overturned; the peace is kept, and the throne is occupied, by thieves. Lawyers and bankers are classified with pickpockets and highwaymen, in Balzac's youthful collection, *Code des Gens Honnêtes*. He supports, with his unexpected authority, the sweeping declaration of the socialist Proudhon that property is theft.

Elements of the factual and the fictitious are so mixed in Balzac's writing that it is never quite certain which will prevail. The progress of his realism was retarded by the competition of such popular romanticists as Dumas and Sue; public apathy persuaded him to abandon the hard actualities of *Les Paysans* for the easy excitations of *Splendeurs et Misères des Courtisanes*. Pornography is by no means excluded from the range of his serious thought. "Prostitution and theft are two living protests, male and female, of the natural state against the social state." Through the darker and dimmer regions of the picaresque and the rocambolesque, we struggle back into the glaring light of comedy; we particularize the generalization that everything has its price, that at heart every man is a thief and every woman a whore, that the *haut monde* is no better than the *demi-monde*. Balzac is better at portraying the fundamental sluttishness of the *grande dame* than at exhibiting the virtuous harlot; his Esthers and Coralies are pallid sisters of Marion Delorme and Sonia Marmeladova.

56

Les Marana argues the superiority of a courtesan to her bourgeois husband. *La Cousine Bette* is dominated by the adventuress, Valérie Marneffe, whose seductive role is the feminine counterpart of Vautrin's, and whose path is strewn with broken families, wasted talents, and spent fortunes. On the other hand we have Adeline Hulot, a paragon of virtue, indignantly rejecting the advances of the boorish Crevel, who resembles a provincial comedian in the role of Tartuffe. But when her husband is ruined by Madame Marneffe, Madame Hulot is compelled to play the seductress—an inept and pitiful performance which offers Crevel his revenge. Rejecting her, he returns to Valérie, and the climactic scene is Valérie's sudden break-down. This, we say,—and our cheap cynicism echoes Balzac's dearly bought shrewdness—is the pay-off:

> *Madame Marneffe left Crevel and knelt again before her chair, clasping her hands in a ravishing posture and repeating with unbelievable unction this prayer: "Ah, Saint Valérie, my kind patron, why don't you visit the bedside of your entrusted child more often? Oh, come this evening, as you came this morning, to inspire me with virtuous thoughts, and I shall leave these evil paths; like Mary Magdalene I shall renounce the misleading delights, the false attractions of the world,—even the one I love so much!"*
>
> *"My sweetie," said Crevel.*
>
> *"Sweetie no longer, Sir!" She turned proudly, like a virtuous woman, and, her eyes wet with tears, she seemed dignified, cold, indifferent. "Leave me," she said, pushing Crevel away. "What is my duty? To belong to my husband. That man is dying, and what am I doing? I am deceiving him on the brink of the grave. He believes your son is his. I am going to tell him the truth, first asking his pardon and then God's. Let us part. Goodbye, M. Crevel," she repeated, rising and holding out an icy hand. "Goodbye, my friend,*

we shall not see each other until we meet in a better world. You have given me some inexcusable pleasures; now I want—yes, I shall have— your respect."

Crevel was weeping warm tears.

"You big fathead," she shrieked, breaking out in infernal laughter. "That's the way these pious women go to work on you to chisel two hundred thousand francs!"

4. THE THIRTY-THIRD MANDARIN

The weakness of the demiurge or megalomaniac, when he takes the trouble to superimpose a cosmos upon his private share of the public chaos, is that he creates a better world, an unrecognizable utopia, a fool's paradise. It is here that Balzac exhibits his strength, by creating a microcosm which— if anything—is worse than this world. Exact reproduction, except in such simple matters as stage properties and scenic effects, is impractical; what the realist must do is to stir his readers out of their preconceived and conventional worlds, if necessary by darkening his pictures and exaggerating his strokes, with the murk of Doré and the sweep of Delacroix. Romanticism thus contributes to realism in the sense that commonplace reality does not, in the Aristotelian sense that poetry is truer than history. Which, after all, is the true Balzac: the porcine face that stares myopically out of Nadar's daguerreotype, or the leonine head that tosses restlessly back from Rodin's colossus? The artist in Balzac, taking his cue from the moralist, goes beyond the scientist and the businessman. When he transubstantiates values into prices, he is not selling out; he is harshly reminding us that there are other standards than gold. For a man who could never make both ends meet, who was capable of making a dowerless marriage, whose intellectual appetites were as vast and undiscriminating as his literary energies, there were more important things than money—or, at any rate, there should have been. What should be, of course, is the province of moralists like Carlyle. But when Carlyle points the moral of the French Revolution or the middle ages, when he preaches hero-worship or the gospel of work, he is adorning a tale which

59

Balzac has already told. And Balzac has graphically illustrated Carlyle's strongest contention: that the *laissez-faire* society of industrial capitalism discounts all obligations except the cash nexus.

It is Balzac's zeal for tracing financial relationships that links cause to effect, plot to character, and volume to volume in the *Comédie Humaine*. Although "the great social force is character," it can only be activated by material forces. Hence sociology comes first and last with Balzac, with psychology crowded in between. "Tell me what you have and I will tell you what you think." Property conditions thought and thought produces action. Balzac begins by telling us what his characters have; their incomes and addresses, their houses and furnishings, their clothes and physiognomies are chosen to fit with unique propriety. He then tells us what they think, with special reference to the pseudo-sciences of mesmerism and phrenology, which provide him with the easiest and most external means of characterization. The influence of one personality upon another—for example, of Vautrin upon Rubempré—is explained away by a kind of hypnosis; and psychological characteristics are manifested through their corresponding physical traits, such as Goriot's hypertrophied bump of paternity. Emotions are so externalized that ladies not infrequently die of love, and fortunes are predetermined by physiognomies. The comic decorum of every man in his humor is preserved by type-casting, and by salting the dialogue with *mots de caractère*. "You are too much of a Marneffe, M. Marneffe," says Baron Hulot. A few pages afterward, when the blackmailing husband has gained the upper hand, he retorts, "You are too much of an Hulot, M. Hulot." So it might be said, of all Balzac's characters, that they are rather too insistently themselves. This egoistic insistence, by selecting in each case the prime specimen of a class, animates a series of stock types with Balzac's driving megalomania. All of them, says Maurice Bardèche, are *avares* and *absents*: avid for something and absent-minded about everything else. Everyone, it seems, is a nonpareil. "Even the janitors' wives," Baudelaire maintains, "have genius."

Balzac describes his method as "individualizing the type and typifying the individual," as lending concreteness to abstractions in the *Etudes Philosophiques* and lending generality to particulars in the *Etudes de Moeurs*. More often than not he proceeds deductively, starting from first principles and picking up incidental details. In *Une Fille d'Eve*, having mentioned the "secret saturnalia of literature and art mingled with politics and finance," where "Desire reigned as a sovereign" and "Spleen and Fantasy were sacred," he proceeds to list the guests, filling in each category with its appropriate representatives. He recruits his cast from the virtues and vices, the talents and interests, by a process of personification. When he characterizes a stalwart peasant as "the Milo of Crotona of the valley," or Vautrin as "the Cromwell of the prison," or Goriot as "the Christ of paternity," he may be establishing what Arnold Bennett calls "a frame of conventionalization." He may, as Professor Curtius suggests, be attributing the most variegated forms of human experience to the same primordial energy. He is also asserting the timelessness of certain historic patterns and moral problems. Concurrently, he is adapting them to his own time. As his work accumulates and his scope enlarges, he discovers objects of comparison in his previous books, and introduces his creations side by side with real people in the walk-on parts. Not Talleyrand but Gondreville is his byword for political intrigue; not Don Juan but Maxime de Trailles is the paragon of erotic dalliance. Balzac, in sum, has created his own mythology, fixing the archetypes of literature and affecting the conventions of society for many years to come. Jules Vallès has left an unforgettable account of the impression Balzac made upon a younger generation whose Amadis de Gaul was Vautrin, whose ambition was to succeed in everything and believe in nothing, who wanted decorations in their buttonholes, duchesses in their arms, and millions in their bank-accounts.

Whether we choose to regard Balzac as a creator of myths, assigning a tutelary genius to every sphere, or as a compiler of statistics, competing with the civil registry, it is not the individuality but the typicality of his characters that stays with us. They do not step out of his books and into our lives, like some of the memorable characters in fiction. Rather it is we who remain detached, while they become increasingly involved in the trammels of circumstance. And circumstance is so many-sided and far-reaching that it transcends the limits of any single volume. The brilliant device that integrates Balzac's volumes, the *retour des personnages*, is not his invention; it is as old as the first writer who hit upon a success and wrote a sequel; it may have been suggested to Balzac by the reappearances of Leatherstocking through five of Cooper's novels. But heretofore no novelist had made it an instrument for catching the facets of personality, for recording the passage of years, for registering the shifts and compromises and realignments that interrelate a series of careers. If psychology added a third dimension to the flat, old-fashioned technique of characterization, Balzac's system of cross-reference added a fourth—the dimension of time and change in which Proust was to move. This discovery was first utilized in *Le Père Goriot*, which gathers up the loose ends of preceding stories and plants the presuppositions for further ones. It proved so suggestive that it seems to have been largely responsible for the extraordinary fruitfulness of Balzac's next few years. It provided him with a backlog for his *dramatis personae*; each minor character demanded a larger part in a new story. *César Birotteau* makes use of 104 reappearing characters and *Illusions Perdues* of 116, by Miss Ethel Preston's reckoning. With *Splendeurs et Misères* no less than 155 old friends put in an appearance, crowding the novel into shapelessness.

Here the law of diminishing returns sets in, and Balzac, drawing less upon his stock-company for his later productions, replenishes his personnel. *Les Parents Pauvres*, comprising his two maturest novels, is almost an afterthought: neither *La Cousine Bette* nor *Le Cousin Pons* has a place in his original plan. They are more self-contained than the earlier installments of the *Comédie Humaine*, which are designedly fragmentary and interdependent. Though Balzac recapitulates and moralizes, he seldom commences or concludes; he is always, like life itself, in the midst of things. Thus *Le Père Goriot* presupposes *Gobseck* and *L'Auberge Rouge*, and is consummated by *La Maison Nucingen* and *Splendeurs et Misères*. And thus, because its continuing interrelationships are more significant than its characters in any given situation, the whole of Balzac's work is greater than the sum of its parts. It is no more than a coincidence that both the alchemist Claës and the perfumer Birotteau should purchase their supplies from the same chemical firm. To recognize Birotteau's brother in *Le Curé de Tours* does no more, perhaps, than underline the generalization that the world is indeed small. But to observe that Eugénie Grandet's lover was swindled by the very notary who precipitated Birotteau's bankruptcy is to score a Balzacian point. And to follow the rise of Birotteau's successor, Célestin Crevel, is to realize the decay of bourgeois standards between the Napoleonic generation and the eighteen-forties. "Do you know whom Félix Vandenesse is marrying?" Balzac once asked his sister. "One of the Granville girls. They are making a fine match. The Granvilles are wealthy, in spite of what that Mlle. de Bellfeuille has cost the family." The reader can watch the outcome of this marriage in *Une Fille d'Eve;* he may trace the gossip to *Une Double Famille;* he will remember Félix' first love from *Le Lys de la Vallée,* and piece together Granville's legal career from half a dozen other novels.

Reading Balzac—plunging in somewhere, trying again elsewhere, putting two and two together, accumulating impressions and implications—approaches the conditions of actual experience more immediately than the usual narrative sequence with a beginning, a middle, and an end. *Les Misérables,* by contrast, is a thin piece of work, thickened by rhetorical and technical devices: every other person turns out to be Thénardier in disguise. Balzac's advantage is grounded on the multiplicity and consistency of his characters. His cross-references, biographically rearranged and alphabetically catalogued by MM. Cerfbeer and Christophe, form a *répertoire* which is scarcely less fascinating or convincing than *Who's Who?* Character is stamped, in each instance, by actions and affiliations, by words rather than thoughts. Except on a behavioristic plane, it cannot be maintained that Balzac's extro-

63

verts offer much opportunity for psychological exploration. Taine's metaphor is crude but not inappropriate, when he dismisses them as pedestals, on which the respective passions are poised like statues. In statuesque repose, in static arrangement, they would be heavy and lifeless; they are brought to life by the interplay of dynamic forces. Balzac's method, to use his own metaphor, is physiological rather than anatomical; he is more concerned with movement than with form. His books are intricately geared together to convey a sense of movement, which in turn conveys the social mobility of the epoch. An apprentice attains the Bourse, a street-walker the Opera. An inventor goes bankrupt, a *grande dame* is seduced. The poet is in debt to the tradesman, who is in debt to the banker, we read in one book; the banker is in love with the courtesan, who is in love with the poet, we read in the next volume. Everything moves in vicious circles, but it keeps moving.

The philosopher of motion, Louis Lambert, investigates the chemistry of the will. The *Avant-propos* sweepingly asseverates that "passion is all humanity." Passion and will, as closely identified with bodily mechanisms as in the James-Lange theory of the emotions, function as stimulus and response in the Balzacian psychology. Will is a kind of avarice or concupiscence, depending upon the nature of its object. Passion is motivated by the object's magnetic attraction. When this motivation is unworldly, artistic or scientific, it usually leads to monomania; when it has a material basis, it is usually connected with money or sex. Business connexions are the usual link between Balzac's *dramatis personae* because business, as the younger Dumas was to note, is "other people's money." Balzac's mode of analysis, equating self-interest with financial interest, ascribes the profit motive,— *Vous êtes orfêvre, M. Josse*—to the butcher, the baker, and the candlestick-maker. As for the other kind of connexion, the sexual liaison, it is even more universal and therefore less characteristic of Balzac. It is the major premise in the *Contes Drolatiques*, where the joke reduces everything to a common denominator of carnality, and the minor premise in the *Comédie Humaine*, where finance is the major. The affairs of the Princesse de Cadignan are no less a cross-section of society than the affairs of the Baron de Nucingen. Where marriage itself is a transaction, as in *Un Contrat de Mariage*, adultery becomes the natural relationship between the sexes, and a scandalously high proportion of Balzac's characters are born out of wedlock. Marriage is treated sociologically, sex physiologically, and a psychological treatment of love completes the triangle in *Le Lys de la Vallée*. This is Balzac's exacerbated commentary on the wavering Platonism of Sainte-Beuve's *Volupté*. The romance of Félix de Vandenesse with the Countess de Mortsauf is as idyllic as Petrarch's with Laura. But the repressed passion reveals itself at her deathbed, and this model of virtuous womanhood dies with ghastly coquetries and obscene imprecations on her lips.

All women, to the lover of Eveline Hanska, were daughters of Eve, from the romantic schoolgirl, Modeste Mignon, to the *sandiste* writer, Camille Maupin. The habit of elopement, in *Une Femme de Trente Ans*, is handed down from mother to daughter. Frequently Balzac protests against Scott's heroines: the chill of the protestant north, he feels, is upon them. Thackeray might archly overlook the open secret of Becky Sharp's charm, referring to her as "that wretched woman," and apologizing for the scales of the mermaid below the water; but Balzac—and along with him, Taine—was frankly swept off his feet by Valérie Marneffe. She is the real protagonist of *La Cousine Bette*. Her accomplice, Lisbeth Fischer, is deadlier than the masculine "poor relation," Sylvain Pons; she is the grasping peasant, the smouldering artisan, "Hatred and Vengeance" personified, "the Mohican whose snares are inevitable." But these snares are set through the gold-digging wiles of Valérie. The comic scene in which Valérie's two middle-aged suitors, Crevel and Hulot, are locked out in the street together is as grimly passionate as that tragic scene in *The Idiot* where Myshkin and Rogozhin are found with the body of Nastasya Filippovna. After Valérie has married Crevel, a terrible retribution overtakes them; yet even in the last stages of a leprous disease, she runs true to type, in her confidence that she will be able to

"get around God." Her principal victim, the Baron Hulot d'
Ervy, survives his dyed whiskers and cast-off corsets, his philander-
ings and fraudulent army contracts, and the ruin of his family,
to descend with each successive mistress into a lower circle of
sensual degradation. To bring home the object-lesson, by way of
Plutarchan parallel, we recognize in his brother, old Marshal
Hulot, the stern young revolutionary soldier of *Les Chouans*.

As the prodigal father, Baron Hulot stands at the apex of
that inverted pyramid which represents, for Balzac and Bonald, an
overturned social hierarchy. "Society—the world—revolves around
fatherhood," exclaims Père Goriot, who is plainly obsessed with
his role as a latter-day Lear, and whose officious paternalism does
not stop short at playing the pandar to his daughters. "Everything collapses when children do not love their parents." His
daughters are too busy to attend his deathbed, and his landlady
is too stingy to waste clean sheets upon a dying man. Nothing
indicates more sharply than these grim death-watches, in which
Balzac seems to delight, the displacement of family ties by the
bonds of interest—particularly when, as in *Ursule Mirouët*, or
Le Cousin Pons, the heirs fall out over the will. *Martin Chuzzle-
wit* is comparatively benign. Concentrating each set of his *études*
upon a different age group, Balzac was already aware of the ten-
sion that would be felt between the generations in the second
half of the century. If the fathers had eaten sour grapes, what
could be expected of the sons? The unprincipled opportunism of
Henri II's maxim: "There is no such thing as absolute virtue;
there are only circumstances." *L'Elixir de Longue Vie is* concocted
of patricide; the unfilial hero-villain, Don Juan, like Faust or Melmoth or Mirabeau or Bonaparte, is an image of evil, more specif-
ically of the individualism that disintegrates families. As he can-
vasses the ranks and crannies of society, Balzac's heart goes out
to the unattached and the celibate, the old maid or the elderly
bachelor, victims of worldly intrigue like the good-natured Abbé
Birotteau or the pathetic slavey Pierette. His Niobe-like mothers,
the Countess de Dey in *Le Réquisitionnaire* or the widow Bridau
in *La Rabouilleuse*, mourn for the children of the century.

66

His real protagonists are the *enfants du siècle*. The main direction of the *Comédie Humaine* is pointed by their careers, contemporary and concurrent with his own. The mediocrities, like Oscar Husson in *Un Début dans la Vie*, live down their legal and military escapades to become solid citizens. "*C'est enfin le bourgeois moderne*," Balzac breaks off with a shrug. A high-principled and highly competent public servant, like Xavier Rabourdin in *Les Employés*, is quite exceptional; his reward is to see incompetents and intriguers promoted above his head. The self-effacing Z. Marcas, his brains picked by unscrupulous politicians, dies prematurely and obscurely. His legacy is a warning: "Pent-up youth will burst out like the boiler of a steam engine." As long as the regime can buy off the rising talents, however, that explosion will be postponed. Two voices beset Lucien de Rubempré on the road to Paris. "Intelligence is the lever that moves the world," cries one. But the other flatly declares that the prop of intelligence is money. And the young poet from the provinces, finding Paris a "lupanar of thought," is faced with the alternative of starving in a garret or coming to terms with the literary market. A "candidate for posthumous honors," an Arthez or another of his Cénacle, may choose the hard way; but Lucien's feet are soon on the primrose path. Having abandoned poetry for journalism, he soon abandons liberal principles for royalist bribes. The moral of *Splendeurs et Misères des Courtisanes* is that the talented writer who sells his mind prostitutes himself more abysmally than the pathetic women who sell their bodies on his behalf. As a devastating study in the ways and means of intellectual prostitution, *Illusions Perdues* is still authoritative and still pertinent.

John Dos Passos has vividly restated the attractions and repulsions of *The Big Money* for the last generation of Americans. Balzac had the advantage of gaging these effects while they were freshly observable, and of appealing to an ethical code which had not been altogether upset by materialism. Stendhal, himself a materialist and a hedonist, could sympathize with his careerist heroes. Balzac's careerists engage our sympathies only through their failures; as they succeed, they become unsympathetic. When we first encounter Eugène de Rastignac, he is the hope of his mother and sisters, who pawn their jewels that he may study law. Two of his fellow boarders at the Pension Vauquer exert their counter-influence upon his eager southern temperament: good and bad angels wrestling over his soul. Vautrin tempts his ambition by framing a duel which leaves Mademoiselle Taillefer an heiress, but Rastignac is honest enough to reject this temptation. Goriot offers love, but his daughters' rejection of his own love is an example which fosters egoism rather than altruism. A lone mourner at Goriot's grave, Rastignac looks down from the cemetery of Père-Lachaise as the lights begin to glitter along the banks of the Seine. The column of Place Vendôme and the cupola of the Invalides define the ground he has chosen for his duel with society. As he goes off to dine with the Baroness de Nucingen, née Goriot, he utters his grandiose challenge: "A nous deux maintenant." Through later volumes we catch glimpses of his social ascent and his rake's progress; finally, in La Maison Nucingen, he makes his killing in the shadiest of stock-market deals and marries the daughter of his old mistress, the Baroness. His political career seems to parallel that of Thiers, who began as a radical leader in the Revolution of 1830, and ended—after putting down the Commune—as first president of the Third Republic.

One of Balzac's favorite walks, during his early explorations of Paris, lay among the tombstones of Père-Lachaise. From the epitaphs he infers, in the preface to Le Vicaire des Ardennes, that the city of the dead reverses the customs of the living metropolis; that here, at any rate, husbands are honest and wives faithful. The cemetery is therefore an appropriate setting for the reversal of values, when Rastignac buries his lost illusions with Goriot and dedicates himself to the main chance. In a case of conscience, borrowed from the master of modern casuistry, Rousseau, he has put the problem to his friend Bianchon. Supposing one could get rich merely by an act of will—merely by willing the death of an aged mandarin in China? "Bah!" is the retort. "I am going on my thirty-third mandarin." When Rastignac insists that the question is serious, Bianchon hesitates, asks the presumable age of the mandarin, and finally renounces the bargain. Dostoevsky, recounting the episode, exaggerates this final renunciation, and forgets the magnificent cynicism of Bianchon's immediate response. For the uncompromising Dostoevsky, no one can be happy while others are suffering. For Balzac compromise is the precondition of happiness, which is invariably paid for by others. Instead of renouncing the bargain, he computes the cost; instead of sparing the mandarins, he reckons the casualties. Bianchon, in spurning Rousseau's hypothetical offer, is more scrupulous than his fellow denizens of the *Comédie Humaine*. Rastignac learns, under the tutelage of Vautrin, to dispense with principles and take advantage of circumstances: "Fortune is virtue." Vautrin's maxim, which placed providence in the hands of the unscrupulous individual, stems from Machiavelli's *Discourses* on the opportunistic policies of Rome. And Rome, as Ben Jonson describes it in *Sejanus*, is not unlike Balzac's Paris:

> *Men's fortune there is virtue; reason, their will,*
> *Their licence, law; and their observance, skill.*
> *Occasion is their foil; conscience, their stain;*
> *Profit their lustre; and what else is, vain.*

These profaner studies in opportunism are counterweighted by *Louis Lambert*, which Yeats has classified as a "sacred book." It is the biography of a schoolmate, sent by Madame de Staël to Balzac's college at Vendôme, where his precocious treatise on the will has been confiscated by their Oratorian masters. After he has graduated, and enlarged his observation of social dynamics, practice continues to frustrate theory. The most serious of Balzac's thinkers, he finds no room for thought in Paris: "Here the point of departure for everything is money." For the *voyant* who refuses to compromise his intellectual integrity, the alternative is madness. His gradual retreat from the Parisian inferno carries him into the visionary sphere of Swedenborg's angels. One of his last unsuccessful acts, the ultimate gesture for a hero who renounces power, is an attempt to castrate himself. Impotence and corruption, the respective destinies of Louis Lambert and Eugène de Rastignac, posed the alternatives of *La Peau de Chagrin*, and testi-

69

fied—for Goethe—to the degeneration of contemporary France. Raphaël de Valentin, another youthful author of a *Théorie de la Volonté*, having gambled away his fortune, is rescued from suicide by an antique dealer, another avatar of the Wandering Jew. The terms of their Mephistophelian contract are embodied in a piece of shagreen, which magically fulfills the wishes of its owner, shrinking slightly—and further curtailing his existence—with every wish. Oscar Wilde, inverting the normal relation between nature and art, has presented the same dilemma in *The Picture of Dorian Grey* and underscored the same implication: that there is no experience which does not exact a heavy price.

Between the desire and the fulfillment, between the appetite and the satiety, between the appearance and reality, Raphaël de Valentin is caught in a Schopenhauerian dilemma of the will. Two words contain the secret of human activity, as revealed to him by the dealer: *Vouloir et Pouvoir . . . Vouloir nous brûle et Pouvoir nous détruit.*" If frustrated ambition consumes his contemporaries, satisfied ambition destroys them. Power corrupts, and the will to power degenerates. Napoleon was undoubtedly "a prodigious phenomenon of the will"; and Julien Sorel may have been, in Nietzschean phrase, "a strong man amid unfavorable circumstances"; but Eugène de Rastignac and Lucien de Rubempré are weak-kneed supermen, who arrive by swimming with the current and flounder whenever they resist it. Rastignac expounds "the morality of the comedy that society plays every day" to Valentin at an orgy, and Valentin concedes that society will henceforth be divided into two parties—resistance and movement. Those who moved with their century would reap, during its middle years, the middle-class satisfactions that M. Homais was so eloquently to express. Those who resisted the march of progress would temporarily be swept aside. But Balzac, a lifelong student of Bonald's *Théorie du Pouvoir*, understood the weakness of power politics. And Nietzsche, whose voluntarism so often reiterates Balzac's, confirmed those paradoxes which reduce the will of the people to anarchy and bestow leadership upon the most adept follower. No reader of Balzac should have been altogether unprepared for the venalities and disillusionments of recent history: even such tired lions as Marshal Pétain or such stupid foxes as Pierre Laval are fabled in the *Comédie Humaine*. Anatole France is not alone, nor without provocation, when he salutes Balzac as "the greatest historian of modern France." For Antonio Labriola he is a more penetrating sociologist than Comte, he is "the actual inventor of class psychology." Edmond and Jules de Goncourt go even farther:

> No one has considered Balzac a statesman, yet he is perhaps the greatest statesman of our time, the only one who plumbed the depths of our ills, who took a long-range view of the disequilibrium of France since 1789, who saw the manners beneath the laws, the facts beneath the words, an anarchy of unbridled interests beneath apparent order, abuses replaced by influences, equality before the law annihilated by inequality before the bench—in short, the delusion of that program of 1789, which has replaced honorable names by five-franc pieces and made noblemen of bankers, and has done nothing else. And it was a novelist who perceived all this.

The novel that prompted this testimonial, *Les Paysans*, has never been popular. Though Balzac considered it his most substantial book, the public response did not encourage him to complete it. It was written to clarify "that terrible social question, . . . that increasingly ardent debate between man and man, between the rich and the poor—" those two nations whose mutual opposition Disraeli had lately proclaimed in *Sybil*. Balzac starts out by meeting halfway the arguments of such literary socialists as Sand and Sue. "We have written poetry about criminals, wept over hangmen, and almost deified the proletarian. . . . Factions have been stirred up, and all their writers cry: 'Workers, arise!' just as the Third Estate was told to arise." Thence the doctor of social medicine proceeds to diagnose the "democratic vertigo" as a permanent conspiracy against property-holders on the part of property-seekers. "This unsocial element, created by the Revolution, will some day absorb the Bourgeoisie, as the Bourgeoisie has devoured the Nobility." On a later page this new force is given the more explicit name of "Communism, that living and acting logic of Democracy." Communists have acknowledged the justice of Balzac's analysis, stern as it is: a Soviet critic, V. Grib, characterizes *Les Paysans* as "the *Cherry Orchard* of French literature." Balzac, however, is less concerned with the nostalgic disintegration of the old regime than with the predatory lawlessness of the new. The estate of Aigues, after harboring the old age of an eighteenth-century opera-singer, passes to a retired Napoleonic general, who is no match for the depradations of tenants and poachers, conniving stewards and village politicians. When the chateau is razed and the estate divided, the revolution has completed itself and the last outpost of feudalism has surrendered. New owners, petty proprietors, rentiers can now move in. *Chacun chez soi!*

Les Paysans has nothing in common with the bucolics of Vergil or the pastoralism of George Sand, and little with the rustic utopianism of the earlier *Scènes de la Vie de Campagne*. Its relentless burden is *Qui terre a guerre a*. Writing shortly before the socialist revolution of 1848, Balzac refers the question of property back to the land itself and to man's primitive warfare over possession. One need not travel to America, remarks the journalist Etienne Blondet, in order to behold Cooper's redskins. "After all, its an Indian's life surrounded by enemies, and I am defending my scalp," announces Vautrin, when he makes his appearance on the stage. "Paris, you see, is like a forest in the new world, agitated by twenty sorts of savage tribes—Illinois and Hurons living on the products of the different social classes," he warns Rastignac in *Le Père Goriot*. "You are hunting after millions." His own role is not so much the diabolical tempter as the frontier guide, who teaches younger men to bait their traps and track their prey, and who blazes a trail through the pathless faubourgs. It is ironic that Fenimore Cooper should have been living in Paris during these very years, trying to recapture the spirit of Natty Bumpo in *Deerslayer* and *Pathfinder*. Meanwhile Balzac has been pursuing his own particular tribe of savages—*mohicans en spencer et hurons en*

72

redingote, as they were designatel by André Le Breton; *Les Mohicans de Paris*, to borrow an epithet from the elder Dumas; or, to employ a more modern designation, *apaches*. Balzac had come a long way since he modelled *Le Dernier Chouan* on *The Last of the Mohicans* or prompted Marche-à-Terre to emulate Magua; but Cooper had come along to suggest epic comparisons for the bourgeoisie and to provide, where civilization breaks down, the harsher backgrounds of nature.

It is the stark antagonism, the brute ferocity, the endless hostilities, so near to the cloying surfaces of the Leatherstocking novels, that account for their continued influence over the *Comédie Humaine*. The poor relation, Lisbeth Fischer, is the Mohican in ambush, the eternal revolutionary. Where Tolstoy idealizes the wisdom of the folk in Platon Karataev,—who coincidentally recounts a warm-hearted Russian version of *l'Auberge Rouge*— Balzac's peasantry is the soul of invidious guile. Not that he is prejudiced against them; for he respects the aristocracy, and yet presents them as debauchees and weaklings. Both the upper and the lower classes debase themselves, in his opinion, by competing with the middle class. Only the dispossessed retain their dignity. After the July Revolution, *Le Curé de Village* maintains, "The only patriotism is found beneath dirty shirts." Balzac, in the end, is to be found on neither side, though he has never been far from the thick of the battle. Rastignac, he tells us, has seen the three great expressions of society: "Obedience, Struggle, and Revolt; the Family, the World, and Vautrin." Goriot exemplifies the domestic virtues; the outlaw speaks for rebellion; between these extremes lies Balzac's worldly path. The middle way, the way of most men, is an uncertain struggle. The uncertainties of Balzac's struggles and their impact on his work can hardly be exaggerated beyond his own description: *lutte, lutte financière, lutte acharnée* are the catchwords of his correspondence. To Countess Hanska he outlined his life as "combat for money, battle against jealousy, perpetual struggle with my subjects, physical struggles, moral struggles." It was, as Victor Hugo agreed, "a life of storms, struggles, quarrels, combats." Even school, for Louis Lambert, is "a continual struggle between teachers and pupils." *Le Curé de Tours* pushes the struggle into the sanctuary of the church. "I must struggle," resolves Lucien de Rubempré, approaching Paris. Not two of Balzac's books, but all of them, might be headed *Les Rivalités*.

As much as life varies, it always remains, in terms of Balzac's early *Code*: "a perpetual combat between the rich and the poor." Balzac was able, while Darwin and Russell were still experimenting, to depict it as a struggle for existence. And, before Marx and Engels had formulated their slogans, Balzac had completed a powerful depiction of the class struggle. Marx was generous in acknowledging the debt, and Gobseck raises his ugly head in a footnote to *Das Kapital*. Engels, writing to an English novelist, confesses to have learned more from Balzac than "from all the professional historians, economists, and statisticians of the period together." This is high praise for a realist—" a greater master of realism than all the Zolas, past, present, and future—" but it is not the highest. The highest must come from a novelist, an imaginative writer of comparable stature and divergent sensibility, who was less involved in the battles of Balzac's time than in the timeless battle waged by God and the devil which turns every heart into a battlefield. Dostoevsky, whose first published work was a Russian translation of *Eugénie Grandet*, had a profound admiration for Balzac and a special insight into his significance: "His characters are the product of the intelligence of the universe! It is not the spirit of the epoch, but of millions of years of struggle, which have ended by producing this result in a human heart." If the fundamental law of drama is conflict—a conflict, as Brunetière argues, of the will—what writer has lodged a stronger bid than the *Comédie Humaine* to establish himself as dramatist of humanity? And what higher tribute can we pay Balzac than to accept the comprehensive title he has so boldly draped over his grand designs and desperate efforts?

74

FOR EARLY PUBLICATION IN

The Sewanee Review

T. S. ELIOT: Milton ● JACQUES MARITAIN: Action: The Perfection of Human Life, and From Existential Existentialism to Academic Existentialism ● JOSEPH FRANK: Balzac and Stendhal ● FREDERICK J. HOFFMAN: The Rhetoric of Evasion ● R. B. HEILMAN: The Unity of King Lear ● BONAMY DOBREE: Mr. O'Neill's Latest Play ● HAROLD H. WATTS: H. D. and the Age of Myth ● GEORGE HAINES IV: Gertrude Stein and Composition ● WILLIAM EMPSON: The Structure of a Complex Word ● PHILIP WHEELWRIGHT: On John Henry Newman ● R. W. FLINT: Four Quartets Reconsidered ● ALBERT CAMUS: Chamfort ● R. JACK SMITH: Intention in an Organic Theory of Poetry ● H. W. HAUSERMANN: W. B. Yeats's Criticism of Ezra Pound ● WALLACE FOWLIE: Mauriac's Dark Hero ● OSKAR SEIDLIN: Hermann Hesse: The Exorcism of the Demon ● HENRI MICHAUX: Selected Poems

Subscription Three Dollars—Single Copies Seventy-five Cents
THE SEWANEE REVIEW, SEWANEE, TENNESSEE

SOME NEW DIRECTIONS BOOKS
OF PERMANENT INTEREST

DYLAN THOMAS — *The Selected Writings.* Poems & Stories. $3.50

JAMES JOYCE — *Stephen Hero.* Autobiographical novel. $3.50
Exiles. His only play. $1.50
James Joyce by Harry Levin. A study. $2.00

ANTHOLOGY — *Contemporary Latin-American Poetry.* $2.50

GARCIA LORCA — *Three Tragedies.* Includes "Bernarda Alba." $3.75
Lorca by Edwin Honig. A study. $2.00

ISHERWOOD — *The Berlin Stories.* Two novels. $3.50

HENRY JAMES — *Stories of Artists and Writers.* $3.50
The Spoils of Poynton. A novel. $1.50

LAUTRÉAMONT — *Maldoror.* The first Surrealist classic. $6.00

ANTHOLOGY — *Spearhead.* 10 years' experimental writing. $5.00

FRANZ KAFKA — *Amerika.* One of his three novels. $1.50
The Kafka Problem. A critical symposium. $5.00

FITZGERALD — *The Crack-Up.* Edited by Edmund Wilson. $3.50

HENRY MILLER — *The Cosmological Eye.* Representative writings. $3.00
The Colossus of Maroussi. About Greece. $3.00
Remember To Remember. His most recent book. $3.75

PAUL VALERY — *Selected Writings.* In Translation. $3.50

EZRA POUND — *Personae.* The collected poems. $3.50
The Cantos. Up through Canto 84. $5.00
Selected Translations. Coming in 1948. $3.75

THOMAS MANN — *The Stature of Thomas Mann.* A Symposium. $5.00

PATCHEN — *The Memoirs of A Shy Pornographer.* $3.00
Selected Poems. $1.50

GOETHE — *Faust.* The MacIntyre Translation. $3.50
Goethe's World. Letters and Pictures. (1949)

W. C. WILLIAMS — *First Act.* Two novels. $3.50
Selected Poems. $1.50

D. H. LAWRENCE — *Selected Poems.* $1.50
The Man Who Died. $1.50

NEW DIRECTIONS BOOKS, 500 Fifth Ave., New York